Process
Pipe Drafting

by

Terence M. Shumaker
Instructor of Drafting Technology
Clackamas Community College
Oregon City, Oregon

South Holland, Illinois
THE GOODHEART-WILLCOX COMPANY, INC.
Publishers

10-90   BT   2200

Library of Congress Cataloging in Publication Data

Shumaker, Terence M.
  Process pipe drafting.
 	
  Includes index.
  1. Chemical plants — Pipe lines — Drawings.
  I. Title.
TP155.5.S519 1985   660.2'83   84-27890
ISBN 0-87006-512-2

INTRODUCTION

PROCESS PIPE DRAFTING is designed to provide you with the basic knowledge needed to create process piping drawings. This write-in text is intended to expose you to the fundamental concepts and techniques used within the process piping industry. Once you have learned these fundamentals, you will be able to create piping drawings that are properly arranged and easily understood. Remember, the first job of the piping drafter is to construct accurate drawings, not to design or engineer parts or systems. Throughout this text, numerous tips and suggestions are given to assist you in laying out accurate piping drawings. Read and take heed.

PROCESS PIPE DRAFTING first introduces you to the components of piping systems (fittings, valves, and equipment). Then, it tells you how to put these together to create the various types of drawings used in the industry. These drawings are presented in the same sequence that they are produced by engineering firms. They are designed to teach you to read, comprehend, and create process piping drawings.

Each chapter of the text is followed by a test, activities, and assignments. Some of the activities and assignments can be done directly in the text, itself; others should be done on drawing paper. Pipefitters, welders, and other craftworkers learning to read piping drawings from this book are encouraged to sketch these exercises as a learning aid. Appendix A presents common abbreviations used within the process piping industry and related fields. Appendix B contains charts of welded fitting and flange specifications. Appendix C consists of data from valve manufacturers' catalogs.

The process piping drafting field is varied and exciting. Three major industries occupy this realm: pulp and paper, petroleum and petrochemical, and food processing. A world of opportunities awaits the drafter with curiosity and initiative. A drafting job can naturally lead to design, engineering, estimating, sales, and construction. However, many drafters continue to draw and do piping design layouts because it is a challenging field with a lot to learn. There is also the possibility for travel.

Whatever road you take, apply the fundamentals presented in this text and enjoy your piping.

Terence M. Shumaker

CONTENTS

Chapter 1

OVERVIEW OF PIPE DRAFTING

Industrial pipe drafting is a field that takes us beyond the tiny fittings and small diameter pipe of household plumbing and into the heavy-duty world of industrial processes. The piping requirements of industry far exceed the limited capacities of plumbing and utility piping. The processes we speak of demand large diameter pipe from 4 in. to 48 in. and even larger.

The companies that render the drawings used to build process piping systems must design and engineer the facility to strict specifications formulated by the client. These specifications are based on production requirements, construction codes, and environmental restrictions. The people who draw the systems designed by the engineers must be trained in the field of process piping drafting and must have a working knowledge of pipe, fittings, valves, pumps, and equipment common to the specific type of process.

This chapter provides a look into the field of industrial pipe drafting: who does it, what it involves, and the requirements of the profession.

PIPING AND PROCESSES

A "PROCESS" is basically a method of doing something to achieve a finished product. An industrial process does just that: creates a final product.

In many industries, the raw materials used to create a product — and the finished products themselves — must be moved from one point to another. This is often done with pipes . . . large diameter pipes.

What do we mean when we say large diameter pipes? Process piping normally is anything 2 1/2 in. in diameter and above. A fairly common range of process piping is from 4 in. to 24 in. in diameter. Basically, pipes must be as large as is necessary to accommodate the volume of production.

Production of what and by whom? Those are good questions. To name a few: petroleum and petrochemical industry; food processing industry; breweries and bottling facilities. All heavily rely on piping. Power plants use large diameter pipe for movement of slurries, fuel, water, chemicals, and steam. The pulp and paper industry utilizes process piping for a majority of its functions. See Fig. 1-1.

The wide range of industrial activities requiring the services of industrial pipe drafters yields a variety of exciting and challenging opportunities. Perhaps a look at the companies that employ piping drafters will help round out our overview of industrial pipe drafting.

Fig. 1-1. Paper mills such as this one employ miles of process piping.
(C-E Power Systems, Combustion Engineering, Inc.)

PROCESS PIPING DRAFTING

Let's follow an idea from its inception to its birth as a piping system. Wolfgang Hornblatz, president of Hornblatz Brewery, decides the time is ripe to expand the brewery. He knows the type of equipment needed for the expansion, but realizes that his in-house engineering department is much too small to tackle such a project. So Mr. Hornblatz hires a consulting engineering firm.

ENTER THE ENGINEERING FIRM

The consultants do an initial study of the proposed process piping system. This yields both a cost estimate and a time frame in which the work is to be completed. Client Hornblatz then decides either to go ahead with the work and accept the estimate as is, or alter it in some way. Then the work begins.

Most process piping systems are either designed by a consulting firm or by the owner's engineering department. Only a few large companies and construction firms retain engineering departments of the size that enables them to handle the headaches of a major expansion.

ENGINEERING COMPANY STRUCTURE

Who are the people that work for these large companies and consulting firms? Four basic groups make up the structure of the company: administrative, clerical, engineering, and drafting personnel. Often drafters and engineers are referred to as the "engineering department." See Fig. 1-2.

Our concern here is with engineering and drafting. Engineering includes the chief engineer, project engineers, technicians, designers, and drafters. The drafting department is further divided. The chief drafter is responsible for the lead drafters (group leaders) who, in turn, supervise the senior, intermediate, and junior drafters.

DRAFTING RESPONSIBILITIES

Engineers provide the design of the system. The drafting department transforms these designs and ideas into working drawings. A team of drafters under the direction of a group leader (all assigned by the chief drafter) coordinate and construct all the necessary drawings for the project.

Beyond normal drawing responsibilities, the

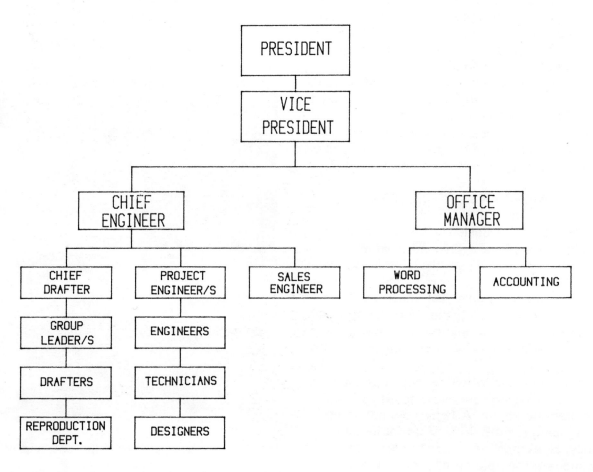

Fig. 1-2. Organization chart of a typical consulting engineering firm shows lines of authority.

drafter may be required to communicate ideas and designs to engineers, designers, clients, and contractors both in person and over the phone. A good working knowledge of freehand sketching is a ''must.'' Where words may fail you, the sketch can save you.

During the project, the drafter may be required to travel to the construction site and perform field work of some sort. This may involve field measurements, locating pipe runs, positioning pumps in an existing morass of equipment, and snooping around sewers with a flashlight seeking the elusive direction of flow.

The drafter may, at those times, be working around machinery and heavy equipment, poking around in underground tunnels, snaking along catwalks high above the mill, crawling amid a maze of piping, Fig. 1-3, or conferring with contractors about the best place for a weld or tie-in. The job of the industrial pipe drafter is potentially one with varied duties, challenges, and problems to be solved.

THE DRAWING SEQUENCE: SITE PLAN

Remember Wolfgang Hornblatz? Well, his initial thought of expansion has now developed into a plan. The project engineers have been assigned. The drafting team is ready to go. Often the first people on the team will create what is called a ''site plan.'' The SITE PLAN is basically a large-scale map of the mill site, showing building outlines, major pipe racks, and possibly large underground pipes. If the facility is existing, the area of expansion will be shown in such a way as to distinguish it from the rest of the mill.

Fig. 1-4 presents an example of a site plan, showing the new area. With this drawing, the client can then decide on changes in the location of the new facility. Keep your erasers hot.

Fig. 1-3. Process piping often appears as a maze.
(CBI Industries, Inc.)

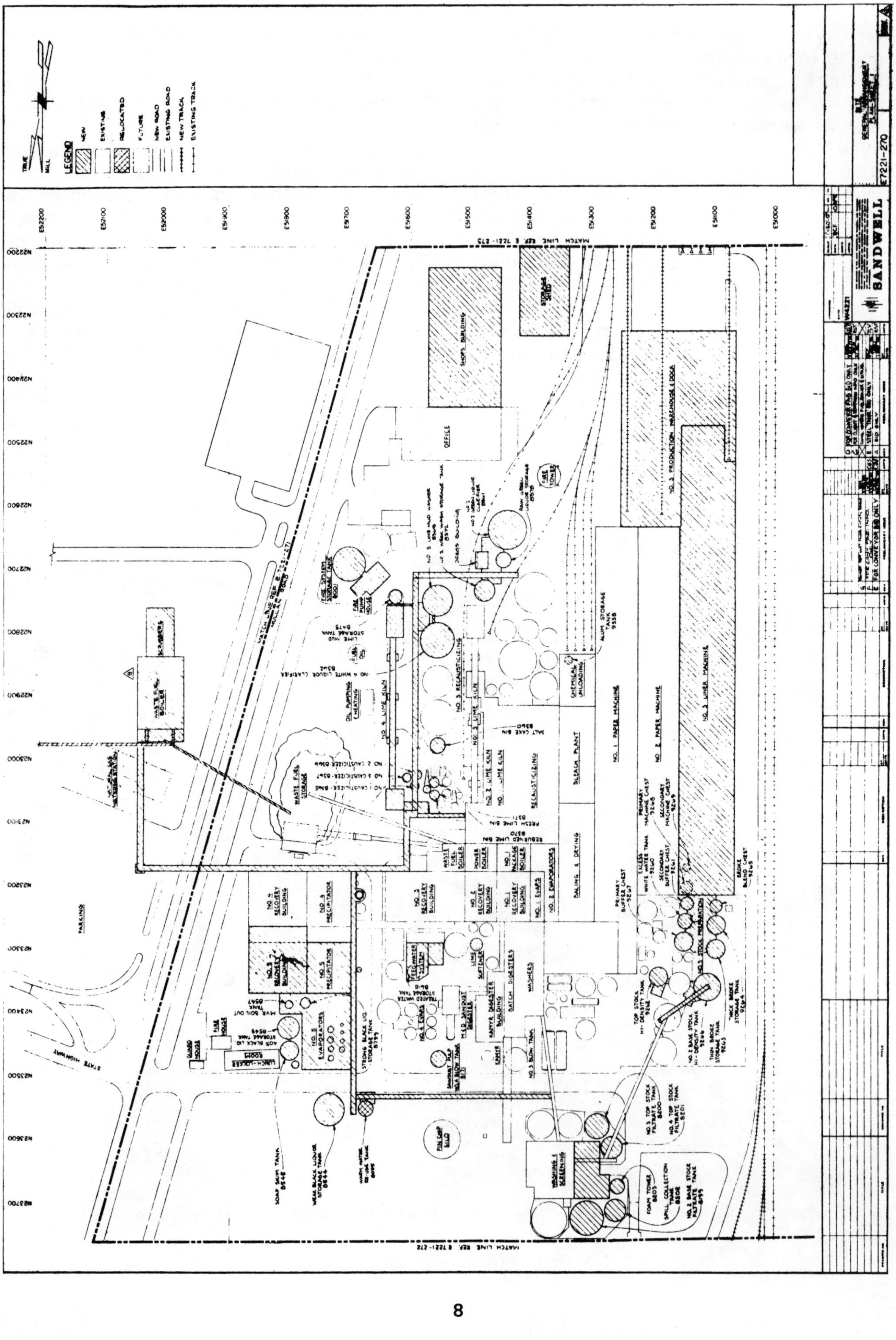

Fig. 1-4. Site plan shows existing facility, along with area of expansion well defined by section lines. (Sandwell International, Inc.)

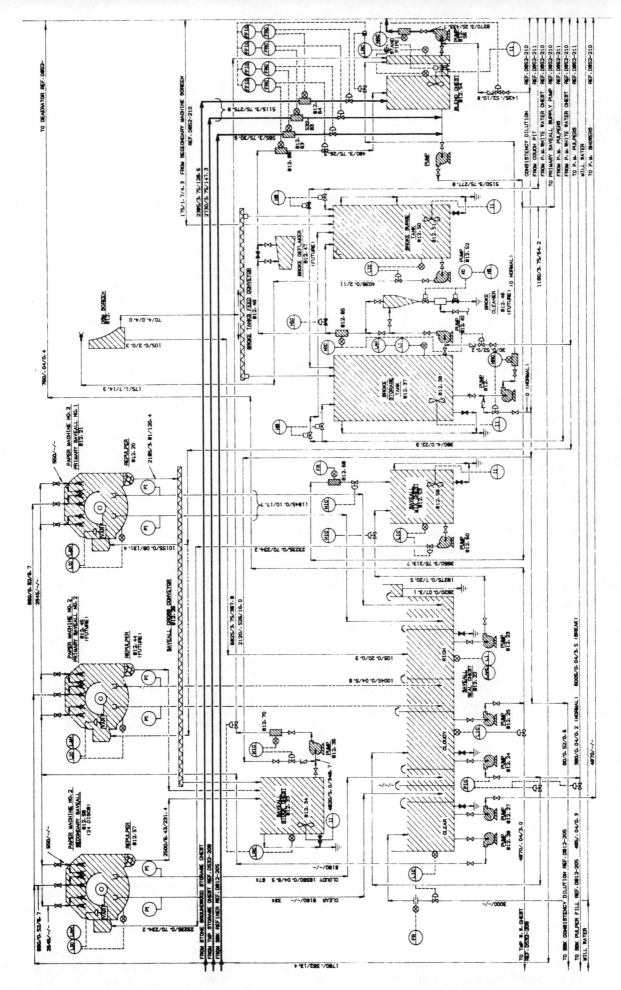

Fig. 1-5. This typical flow diagram reveals entire process piping system at a glance. It is computer drawn. (Sandwell International, Inc.)

FLOW DIAGRAM

While the executives are busy changing their minds about the location of the process piping system, drafters are depicting it on a drawing termed a "flow diagram." The FLOW DIAGRAM is a valuable schematic view of the system that is not drawn to scale. Using symbols, it provides a representation of the entire system, Fig. 1-5.

GENERAL ARRANGEMENT

Once new buildings have been sized and located, they are designed and engineered by the structural department. The piping drafters then use these drawings as background for the general arrangement. The GENERAL ARRANGEMENT drawing shown in Fig. 1-6 reveals the building outline, wall thicknesses, steel columns, equipment locations, and centerline dimensions. The general arrangement is useful in locating equipment, major piping runs, electrical conduit racks, and heating and ventilating ducts.

PIPING DRAWINGS

When equipment locations are decided upon, work begins on piping drawings. PIPING DRAWINGS are composed of plans and sections. They are the heart of any piping system. The PLAN is the view from above and the SECTION is basically a side view of the piping system. The greatest amount of piping drafting time is spent creating these drawings. Fig. 1-7 is an example of a piping plan and section.

ISOMETRICS AND SPOOLS

Two other types of drawings occasionally drawn by the engineering firm — but most often done by the contractor or client — are isometrics and spools. The PIPING ISOMETRIC is a pictorial representation of a single run of pipe. Fig. 1-8 illustrates an isometric. The SPOOL DRAWING is an orthographic subassembly of a portion of the pipe run. Fig. 1-9 shows one of the spools taken from the isometric in Fig. 1-8.

The client's idea is now in the form of spool drawings that will be used by pipefitters to construct the process piping system. But wait. What happens if Hornblatz wants to change his mind? And he will. These changes in the spool drawings are called "revisions."

REVISIONS AND THE DESIGN PROCESS

No introduction to piping drafting would be complete without a glimpse at revisions — the one aspect that eventually comes to haunt even the most meticulous and conscientious drafter. REVISIONS include changes, deletions, and corrections.

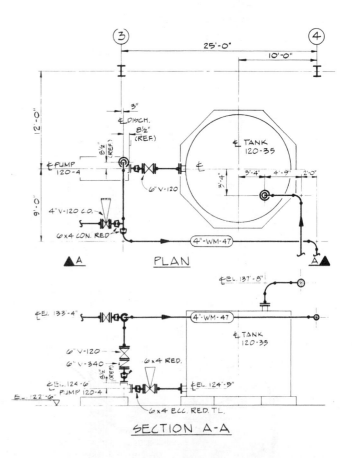

Fig. 1-7. A piping drawing consists of a piping plan (top view) and section (side view).

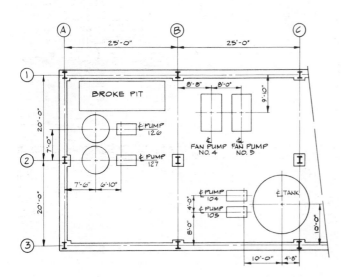

Fig. 1-6. A general arrangement is a dimensioned drawing of building outlines and location of equipment within.

You might add "frustrations." This is mentioned so you will be aware of revisions, their habits, and the nature of the profession that fosters them.

Let's look briefly at the process in which you will be involved. Engineering firms design and create systems, among other things. Beginning as an idea,

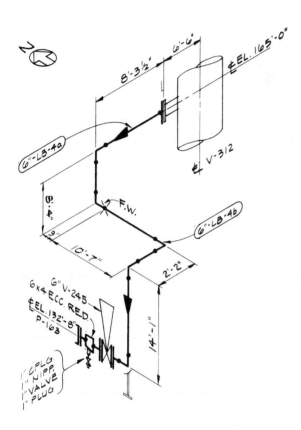

Fig. 1-8. A piping isometric drawing pictures a single run of pipe.

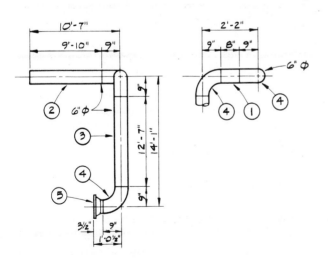

Fig. 1-9. Spool drawing shows a subassembly taken from pipe run in Fig. 1-8. Can you find spool piece in isometric view?

the design is verbalized, possibly written down lest it be forgotten. After initial acceptance by the decision makers, the idea is then transferred to paper in the form of a drawing. This could be a flow diagram, a site plan, or an architectural elevation.

Now the changes begin. An idea is easy to revise once it is on paper. So changes are made, and that creates a revision.

Beyond initial design changes, revisions may be required for a number of reasons. The client may make a change. The vendor's equipment may change. A drafter or engineer may have made an error. Whatever the reason, you — the piping drafter — will be required to draw revisions and obliterate sizable portions of your original work. Hence your need to also possess a good working knowledge of erasing techniques. See Fig. 1-10.

Regardless of the reasons for the revisions, it would be in the best interest of every present and potential drafter to exercise care and conscience on the job. Mistakes are waste.

LINES

You have studied the basics of pipe drafting, the drawing sequence, and drafting responsibilities. Now let's look at the "lines" you will be drawing. The lines do not differ much from those used in mechanical drafting, but their uses and applications may vary. As you read the description and function of each line you will be using on piping drawings,

Fig. 1-10. Eraser is a vital drafting tool, especially when drawing revisions.

refer to Fig. 1-11 and familiarize yourself with line weights and makeup.

CENTERLINE — The thinnest line you will use, it represents the center of equipment and pipes. It is used on all drawings except flow diagrams.

PHANTOM — Another thin line that resembles the centerline except for the extra dash. Found on all drawings, it outlines movable parts, or future pipes or equipment.

SECTION — Thin-to-medium weight lines used to indicate an object or material that has been cut through. Drawn at an angle, they are used on piping elevations.

HIDDEN — A thin-to-medium line indicating features hidden from view. It is used on all drawings.

EXTENSION AND DIMENSION — Thin-to-medium weight lines used to extend features and give dimensions to those features. They are used on all drawings except flow diagrams.

LONG BREAK — A thin line with a Z or "squiggle" inside that indicates a break. It is used for large objects on all drawings.

SHORT BREAK — This line should be as thick as the object line. It indicates a broken part and is used for clarity on the drawing. It is often used on piping details, sections, and tank drawings.

OBJECT — A medium-to-thick line used for the visible lines of equipment, pipe, structural features, etc. It is used on all drawings.

FLOW — The PRIMARY FLOW line is thicker than object line weight. It is used for major flow lines. The SECONDARY FLOW line is similar to an object line in thickness. It represents minor flows. Both flow lines are used on P & I diagrams and flow diagrams.

CUTTING PLANE — Thicker than a primary flow line, it indicates a plane at which the piping can be viewed in elevation. Used on general arrangements and plans.

MATCH — A very thick line employed as a reference for aligning two drawings. It is used on piping drawings, flow diagrams, and general arrangements.

DRAWING QUALITY

Piping drawings are the finished product of an engineering firm much as an engine part is the finished product of a machine shop. Thought, care, and neatness should be applied to any drawing you work on, and careful attention should be given to your company's standards. Several people may work on the same drawing at different times. If standards are adhered to, the result will be a consistent, pleasing drawing. If not, a chaotic

hodge-podge of styles and variations may result. Read the standards and apply them to your work.

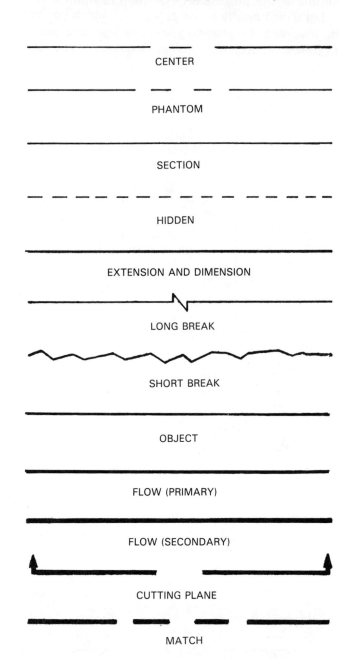

Fig. 1-11. These various types of lines are used in pipe drafting, as well as in mechanical drafting.

DRAWING CLARITY

Don't crowd the information presented on the drawing. Give it some room. Is it easily read? Is it understandable? Could it be placed somewhere else? Ask yourself these questions as you construct a drawing. If something doesn't look right, or appears cluttered, move it somewhere else. Take time to think about the placement of everything you put on the drawing.

Many companies are creating their process piping drawings with computer aided drafting (CAD) systems. These systems produce neat, consistent drawings. The computer drafting systems eliminate the need to concentrate on line quality and lettering style. But these systems do not automatically produce a drawing with a balanced uncluttered layout. That is still the job of the drafter.

Achieving drawing clarity applies to both manual and computer drafting. Developing the ability to produce a balanced, easily understood drawing takes time and practice. As you do the problems in the text, either manually or on a computer, remember that *you* are constructing the drawing. The layout and balance of your piping drawing can be just as easily destroyed with a computer as it can with a pencil. You are in control, and you *can* produce a quality drawing with a balanced and ordered layout. To accomplish that means real job security.

REVIEW QUESTIONS

1. What three factors govern the design of a plant employing process piping? _____
    _____
    _____

2. What is a "process"? _____
    _____
    _____

3. What is a common size range of process piping?
    a. 2 1/2 in. to 12 in.
    b. 4 in. to 24 in.
    c. 4 in. to 48 in.

4. What type of companies design process piping systems? _____

5. Engineers design the process piping system. The drafting department transforms these designs and ideas into _____ drawings.

6. Since the industrial pipe drafter may be required to communicate ideas, a good working knowledge of _____ is a "must."

7. The _____ is basically a large-scale map showing building outlines, major pipe racks, and large underground pipes.
    a. General arrangement.
    b. Site plan.
    c. Plan view.

8. The _____ diagram is a schematic view of the entire process piping system that is not drawn to scale.

9. In piping drawings, the _____ is the view from above. The _____ is basically a side view of the piping system.

10. What is a piping isometric? _____
    _____
    _____

11. What is a spool drawing? _____
    _____
    _____

12. _____ include changes, deletions, and corrections.

13. What type of drawing reveals the building outline, wall thicknesses, steel columns, equipment locations, and centerline dimensions?
    a. General arrangement.
    b. Site plan.
    c. Plan view.

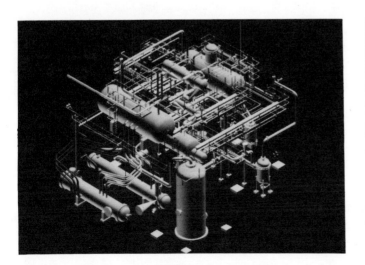

Complex piping layouts, like the one displayed on this terminal, can be designed on a computer-aided design and drafting (CADD) system. Individual drawings can then be generated from the design. (Computervision Corp.)

Name the following lines:

14. _____

15. _____

16. _____

17. _____

18. _____

19. _____

20. _____

PROBLEMS

PROB. 1-1. Write a report on the path of a drawing from its beginnings as an idea to its final use on the job. Contact consulting engineering firms or construction companies or the engineering departments of large process plants.

PROB. 1-2. Prepare a report on the progression of the different types of drawings created by a consulting firm from the initial design of a system to erection.

PROB. 1-3. Conduct a survey and tabulation of companies in your area presently doing process piping drafting, and those using process piping in their manufacturing processes. Contact both designers and users. These could be prospective employers.

PROB. 1-4. Create a flow chart showing the progression of an idea from the design stage through the proper sequence of drawings to the final product.

Note extensive use of piping, fittings, and flanges in this vacuum pump installation. (Fuller Co., Bethlehem, PA)

Pneumatic conveying system at a chemical plant incorporates a maze of pipe runs. (Fuller Co., Bethlehem, PA)

Chapter 2

PIPE AND FITTINGS

PIPE is the medium through which fluid travels. Because there are many types of fluids in varying situations (pressure, acidity, temperature, etc.), there are just as many varieties of pipe. Galvanized, copper, mild steel, cast iron, stainless steel, plastic, fiberglass, concrete, clay, and wood are the basic types. They range in nominal size from 1/2 in. to 36 in. in diameter. Specific situations may call for smaller or larger sizes, or material of a special type.

PIPE SIZING AND SPECIFICATIONS

NOMINAL PIPE SIZE, or NPS, is a common term. All pipe is referred to by the NPS. This size is not always the same as the internal pipe bore. Sizes up to and including 12 in. in diameter have internal bores (inside diameter or ID) equal to their NPS. See Fig. 2-1. Pipe that is 14 in. in diameter and above has an NPS equal to the outside diameter (OD). Therefore, a 6 in. pipe would have an ID of 6 in., and a 24 in. pipe would have an OD of 24 in.

Pipe wall thicknesses vary according to the operating temperature and pressure requirements of the system. Thickness for pipe is indicated most commonly by two standards. The American National Standards Institute (ANSI) classifies by schedule numbers (Sch. 40, Sch. 80, etc.), whereas the American Society of Mechanical Engineers (ASME) and the American Society for Testing and Materials (ASTM) uses the designations ''STD'' (standard), ''XS'' (extra strong), and ''XXS'' (double-extra strong).

Always subtract the pipe wall thickness from the OD to find the ID. Stronger pipe may have an ID less than the NPS. For example, 8 in. schedule 80 pipe has a wall thickness of .500 in. The OD of 8 in. pipe is 8.625 in. By subtracting one inch from 8.625 in., we see that the ID is only 7.625 in. This is a good example of why ''Nominal Pipe Size'' (NPS) is used.

Fittings are also classified according to pressure rating (PSI). Common ratings for buttwelded fittings and flanges are 150# to 600#, and for screwed steel 2000# to 6000#. The strength of pipe and fittings is determined by the conditions (pressure, temperature) under which it will be used.

METHODS OF JOINING PIPE

There are many ways that pipe can be joined. This text deals with welded and screwed piping, the most frequently used methods in industry.

The type of connection used depends on the type and size of pipe. The principle methods include welded, screwed, socketweld, glued, soldered, flanged, and mechanical. Let's take a brief look at a few of the most popular methods of joining pipe.

BUTTWELDED

The BUTTWELD is the most common type of connection found in industry. It is also the most economical and leak-proof method of joining larger diameter piping. Lines that are two inch and larger

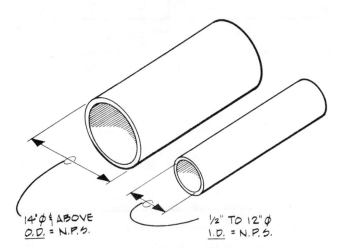

Fig. 2-1. Nominal pipe size (NPS) measurements are based on pipe inside diameter (ID) up to 12 in. and on pipe outside diameter (OD) for 14 in. and larger.

usually are buttwelded. Fig. 2-2 is a chart of the four principal joining methods. Take time to become familiar with these symbols. We'll use some of them later.

SOCKETWELDED

The difference between socketwelding and buttwelding is that in SOCKETWELDING, the pipe is inserted into a socket in the fitting and then welded. In BUTTWELDING, pipe and fittings are "butted" together and then welded. Socketwelding is used primarily on lines smaller than 2 in. when the absence of leaks is critical. Socketwelded joints are used on — but not restricted to — toxic, flammable, or radioactive materials.

SCREWED

The familiar, time-tested method of SCREWED pipe and fittings can be seen in your house plumbing. In industry, it is used for service lines, utility piping, and occasionally for small process piping. Forged steel fittings are used more than cast iron because of their greater mechanical strength. Make note of the symbol for screwed piping in Fig. 2-2. Some companies use the screwed symbol to indicate socketwelded pipe, while others use the buttweld symbol. It always pays to be familiar with your company standards or the job specifications for the project you're working on.

FLANGED

Flanges bolted face-to-face (F to F) with a gasket between the two faces comprise the FLANGED JOINT. A flange basically is a circular piece of steel plate with a machined face and equally spaced bolt holes drilled through it. The large hole through the center of the flange matches the pipe diameter for which it is designed.

Several types of flanges exist, but we'll discuss those a little later in this chapter. Flanges serve to attach valves (and some instruments) to welded pipe or to create removable sections of welded pipe.

PIPE REPRESENTATION

Pipe can be illustrated two ways: as a double line or as a single line. Single line drawing is faster, done manually, but the advent of computer drafting has seen the emergence of more double line piping drawings. Both methods are used in industry, and you should become familiar with the fundamental

aspects of each. One aspect of considerable importance to the drafter is the pipe break. So let's check out the appearance of pipe . . . whole and broken.

PIPE JOINING METHODS

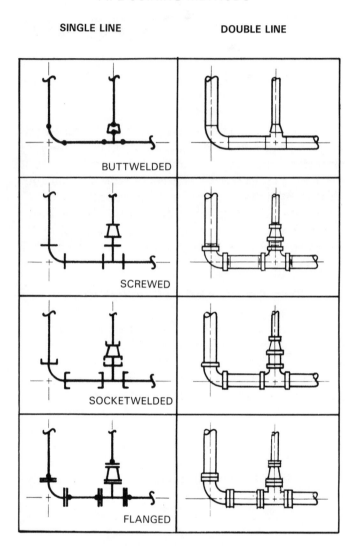

Fig. 2-2. Chart shows various pipe joining methods in single line and double line drawings.

DOUBLE LINE PIPING

Fig. 2-3 gives you a glimpse of this easily understood DOUBLE LINE method of drawing pipe. It looks real. That's why many people would rather draw it or read blueprints employing it. However, it takes longer to draw manually. Some firms show new piping in single line and existing pipe as double line. Others use double line for pipe over 12 in. NPS. Then there are companies that use double line for most everything.

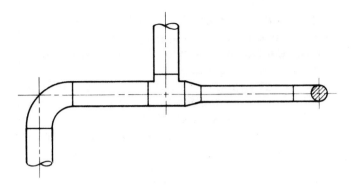

Fig. 2-3. Simple double line piping drawing gives realistic pipe representation.

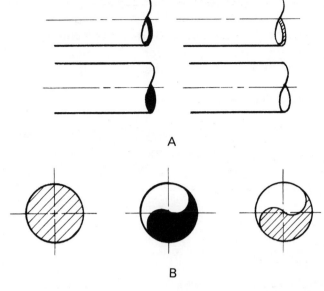

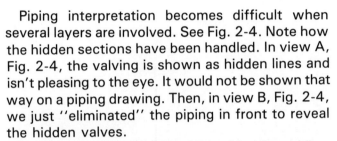

Fig. 2-5. Double line pipe break symbols are illustrated. A — Side view. B — End view.

Piping interpretation becomes difficult when several layers are involved. See Fig. 2-4. Note how the hidden sections have been handled. In view A, Fig. 2-4, the valving is shown as hidden lines and isn't pleasing to the eye. It would not be shown that way on a piping drawing. Then, in view B, Fig. 2-4, we just "eliminated" the piping in front to reveal the hidden valves.

Pipe breaks can be handy things. Use them. View A in Fig. 2-5 is a sampling of double line pipe breaks.

View B illustrates the common methods of showing a broken pipe from the end view; a view often seen in piping elevations. The first example in view

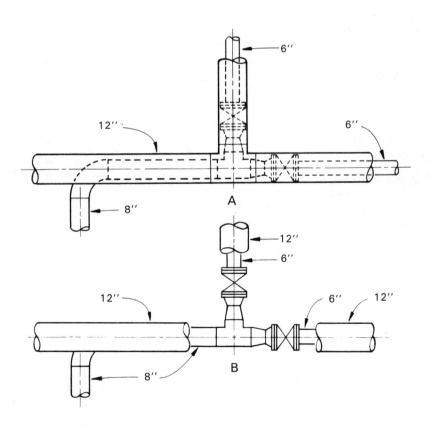

Fig. 2-4. Pipe and fittings are shown in double line drawings. A — Hidden lines indicate hidden section. B — Piping in front is cut away. Note pipe breaks.

B, Fig. 2-5, uses the standard sectioning lines. The second example should be familiar to you "mystics." It resembles the Yin and Yang symbol of ancient Chinese philosophy. The third example is a cross between the other two.

SINGLE LINE PIPING

The SINGLE LINE method of pipe illustration utilizes the centerline of the piping. Fig. 2-6 is a rerun of Fig. 2-3, but is shown in single line. Pipe fades away and fittings suddenly aren't as distinctive as they were on double line drawings. Not quite as easy to read is it? Fear not; just keep referring to the single line fitting symbols in Figs. 2-33 and 2-34 and you'll catch on.

While we're comparing methods, let's look at the single line version of Fig. 2-4. Note how uncluttered and cleaner the piping looks in Fig. 2-7. This becomes an attractive aspect because single line requires less drawing time and provides more open space for dimensions and notations.

Take note of the PIPE BREAKS in Fig. 2-7. They are drawn as a shallow "S" and are actually one half of the double line symbol. Proper construction of break symbols is important. Many a blueprint reader has cursed the improper usage of break symbols. Fig. 2-8 illustrates single and double line break symbols.

Remember, the break symbol is drawn on the nearest pipe. Which pipe is closer to you in Fig. 2-9? If a lower pipe is obstructed by a higher one, it would appear as shown in Fig. 2-10. Which pipe is lowest in Fig. 2-10?

TERMINOLOGY

At this point in your study of piping, a few terms should be introduced. Two of them are used to iden-

tify vertical runs of pipe. A RISER is a vertical pipe in which the fluid is flowing up. A DOWNCOMER is a vertical pipe in which the fluid is flowing down. The third term is used in conjunction with an assembly of fittings and is FITTING TO FITTING. This means that an assembly has no straight pipe, only fittings. So if you see a note that reads "Fitting to fitting riser," you will know what it means.

PIPE FITTINGS

Pipe comes in straight sections, normally 20 ft. lengths. But pipe — like humans — can't go straight forever. It must change direction, change size, or branch out. Enter fittings, which permit the

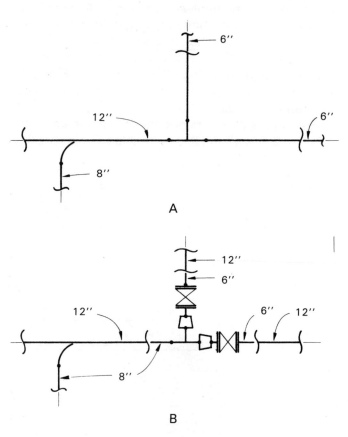

Fig. 2-7. This is a single line version of double line drawings presented in Fig. 2-4. Note use of pipe breaks.

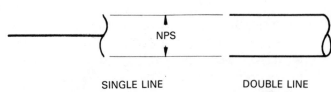

Fig. 2-8. Drawings show proper construction of break symbols.

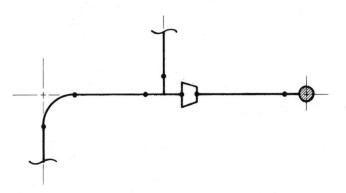

Fig. 2-6. Single line drawing of piping makes use of symbols (see Fig. 2-33) and centerline of piping.

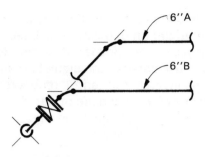

Fig. 2-9. Visualization exercise: Pipe run A is closer to you than pipe run B. Note break symbol at far left of closer pipe run A.

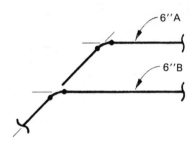

Fig. 2-10. Visualization exercise: Pipe run B is closer to you than pipe run A. Note break symbol at far left of closer pipe run B.

above changes. Let's examine some of the characteristics of pipe fittings.

BUTTWELDED FITTINGS

Fig. 2-11. 90° elbow. (ITT Grinnell)

90° ELBOW: This is the most common "ell" in the extended family of elbows. It permits a 90° change of direction in the pipe run. The most widely used version is referred to as "long radius" (LR). The centerline radius is 1 1/2 times the nominal pipe size (NPS) of 3/4 in. and larger pipe.

Fig. 2-12. 45° elbow. (ITT Grinnell)

45° ELBOW: A close relative of the 90° ell, this fitting allows for a 45° change in the pipe run. Again, the centerline radius is 1 1/2 times the NPS.

Fig. 2-13. Reducing elbow. (ITT Grinnell)

REDUCING ELBOW: Not only does this fitting create a 90° bend, but in the process changes line size. Here, too, the centerline radius is 1 1/2 times the NPS of the *larger* end.

Fig. 2-14. 180° return. (ITT Grinnell)

180° RETURN: This fitting produces a 180° bend. The centerline-to-centerline dimension is 3 times the NPS of 3/4 in. and larger pipe. The 180° return is often used on tank vent stacks or for heating and cooling coils. Two 90° LR ells are often used in place of a return.

Fig. 2-15. 90° elbow (short radius). (ITT Grinnell)

SHORT RADIUS 90° ELL: The only difference between this fitting and the 90° LR *is* the centerline radius, which is equal to the NPS. These ells are used where space is limited.

Fig. 2-16. Straight tee. (ITT Grinnell)

STRAIGHT TEE: A 90° branch from the main run of pipe can be created with a tee. The branch is the same size as the run when a straight tee is used, but a REDUCING TEE produces a branch smaller than the run pipe.

Fig. 2-17. Reducers: A — Eccentric. B — Concentric. (ITT Grinnell)

REDUCER: This fitting joins pipe of differing sizes. It can also be referred to as an increaser, depending on the direction of flow. Two types are

used: CONCENTRIC and ECCENTRIC. The eccentric reducer is flat on one side. It is used when the top or bottom of the pipe must remain level. The drafter must use care when calculating dimensions or elevations involving eccentric reducers, because the centerlines of each end are offset. To obtain this offset, use the formula given in Fig. 2-18.

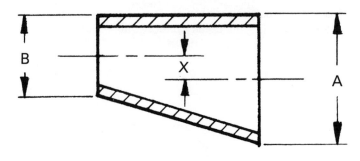

$$X = 1/2 \ (A-B)$$

Fig. 2-18. Eccentric reducer offset formula.

Fig. 2-19. 45° lateral. (ITT Grinnell)

LATERAL: The straight lateral fitting permits 45° entry into the run pipe where the least amount of flow resistance is desirable. The branch diameter is equal to the run diameter. The REDUCING LATERAL has a smaller branch diameter than the run pipe.

Fig. 2-20. Cross. (ITT Grinnell)

CROSS: This fitting provides two 90° branches. Tees and other branching methods are preferred, since crosses are expensive and seldom used except where space is restricted.

Fig. 2-21. Cap. (ITT Grinnell)

CAP: The cap is used to seal the end of the pipe. It is used where the seal will be permanent, such as the end of manifolds and headers.

BUTTWELDED BRANCH FITTINGS

Branch lines are often required on the run pipe. Standard fittings, such as the tee, cross, and lateral, permit certain size and angle branches. However, other, less expensive methods and fittings exist to create branches smaller than the pipe run.

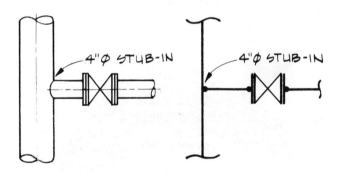

Fig. 2-22. Stub-in.

STUB-IN: This term describes a branch pipe welded directly into the main pipe run. The stub-in is *not* a fitting, but takes the place of expensive fittings such as a tee. The stub-in is used frequently and also is known as a ''nozzle weld'' because it is a common method of producing tank nozzles. Stub-ins are used on 2 in. pipe and larger. Full size pipe and smaller can be welded or ''stubbed-in'' to the main run. When the term ''full size'' is used in piping, it refers to the diameter of the main pipe run.

Therefore, a full size stub-in on a 6 in. pipe would be a branch of 6 in. in diameter.

Fig. 2-23. Welded saddle. (ITT Grinnell)

A piece of shaped metal is often welded over the stub-in joint for extra strength. This creates a WELDED SADDLE as shown in Fig. 2-23. The saddle is a purchased fitting. A PAD can be manufactured at the job site and is often used in place of a saddle.

A little group of buttwelded fittings known as the O'LET family are handy for producing branches at various points. A hole of the required size is drilled or cut into the run pipe, and the O'let branch fitting is welded on. The O'let family is not of Irish descent. A few introductions are in order:

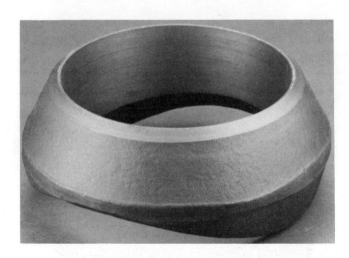

Fig. 2-24. Weldolet. (Bonney Division, Gulf + Western)

WELDOLET® : This fitting makes a 90° branch on run pipe. The branch can be full size or smaller.

The weldolet has threaded and socketwelded counterparts. They are known as — you guessed it — ''threadolet® '' and ''sockolet® .''

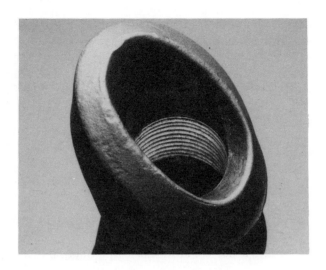

Fig. 2-25. Elbolet. (Bonney Division, Gulf + Western)

ELBOLET® : This strange member of the O'let clan provides reducing branches tangent to 90° elbows.

Fig. 2-26. Latrolet. (Bonney Division, Gulf + Western)

LATROLET® : This fitting makes a 45° branch on straight pipe. The branch will be smaller than the run pipe.

FLANGES

Two basic types of flanges have received wide popularity. They are SLIP-ON and WELDING NECK. Close relations to these are the REDUCING FLANGE, EXPANDER FLANGE, and LAP JOINT. Flanges are primarily used to bolt valves to pipe, and as tank and equipment nozzles. A gasket of an asbestos or rubber compound is always placed between two flange faces to insure a leak-proof seal.

Fig. 2-27. Welding neck flange. (ITT Grinnell)

WELDING NECK: Uses of this flange include tank and equipment nozzles and bolt-up of valves placed next to fittings. When used in the latter situation, the long neck provides strength in the assembly and space for the welding operation.

Fig. 2-28. Slip-on flange. (ITT Grinnell)

SLIP-ON: These are used to flange pipe. Valves located in a pipe run would be mounted with a slip-on flange. These flanges are so named because they actually slip over the end of the pipe. Two welds are required on the slip-on as compared to one on the weld-neck.

Fig. 2-29. Expander flange. (Tube Turns)

REDUCING AND EXPANDER: These two flanges are used in place of a flange and a reducer, but not as a rule. Always check the project specifications before using these flanges and any other odd fittings.

LAP JOINT: Also known as a "Van Stone" flange, this hybrid is normally used on expensive pipe such as stainless steel. It is composed of two parts, the "stub end" and the flange. Only the stub end need be stainless. The flange can be carbon steel. NOTE: "Stub end" should not be confused with "stub-in."

Fig. 2-30. Lap joint flange. (ITT Grinnell)

Fig. 2-32. Blind flange. (ITT Grinnell)

Fig. 2-31. Lap joint flange, stub end. (ITT Grinnell)

BLIND FLANGE: This flange creates a temporary seal on the end of the pipe. It is used where future expansion is anticipated.

SCREWED FITTINGS

Screwed pipe and fittings are available in sizes from 1/8 in. to 4 in., but the maximum size normally used is 2 in. Most of the fittings previously described have their threaded cousins. Fig. 2-34 provides the symbols used for screwed fittings.

Socketweld and threaded fittings. (Bonney Forge Div., Gulf & Western Co.)

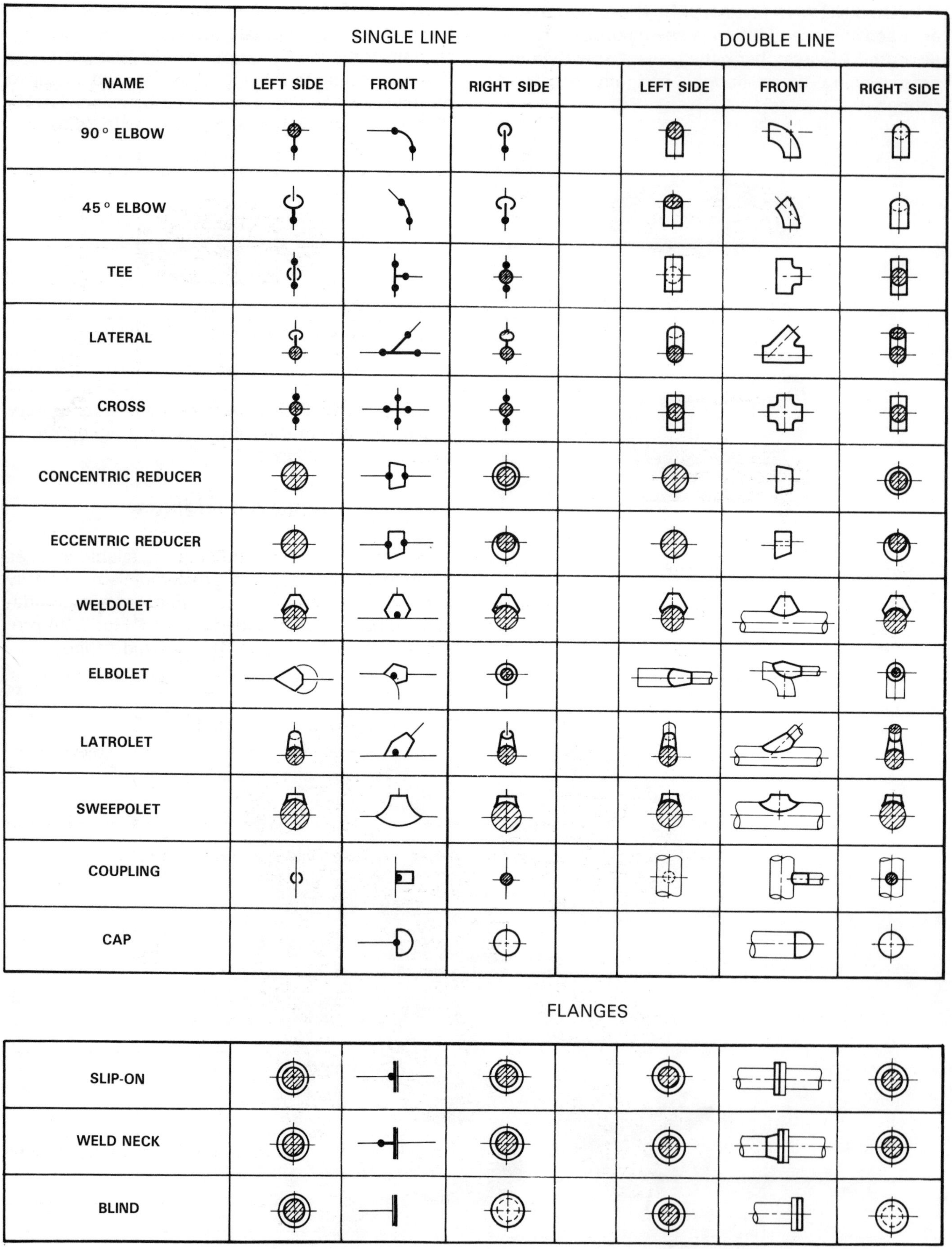

| | SINGLE LINE | | | | DOUBLE LINE | | |
NAME	LEFT SIDE	FRONT	RIGHT SIDE		LEFT SIDE	FRONT	RIGHT SIDE
90° ELBOW							
45° ELBOW							
TEE							
LATERAL							
CROSS							
CONCENTRIC REDUCER							
ECCENTRIC REDUCER							
WELDOLET							
ELBOLET							
LATROLET							
SWEEPOLET							
COUPLING							
CAP							

FLANGES

SLIP-ON							
WELD NECK							
BLIND							

Fig. 2-33. This chart shows three views of single line and double line buttwelded pipe fitting symbols.

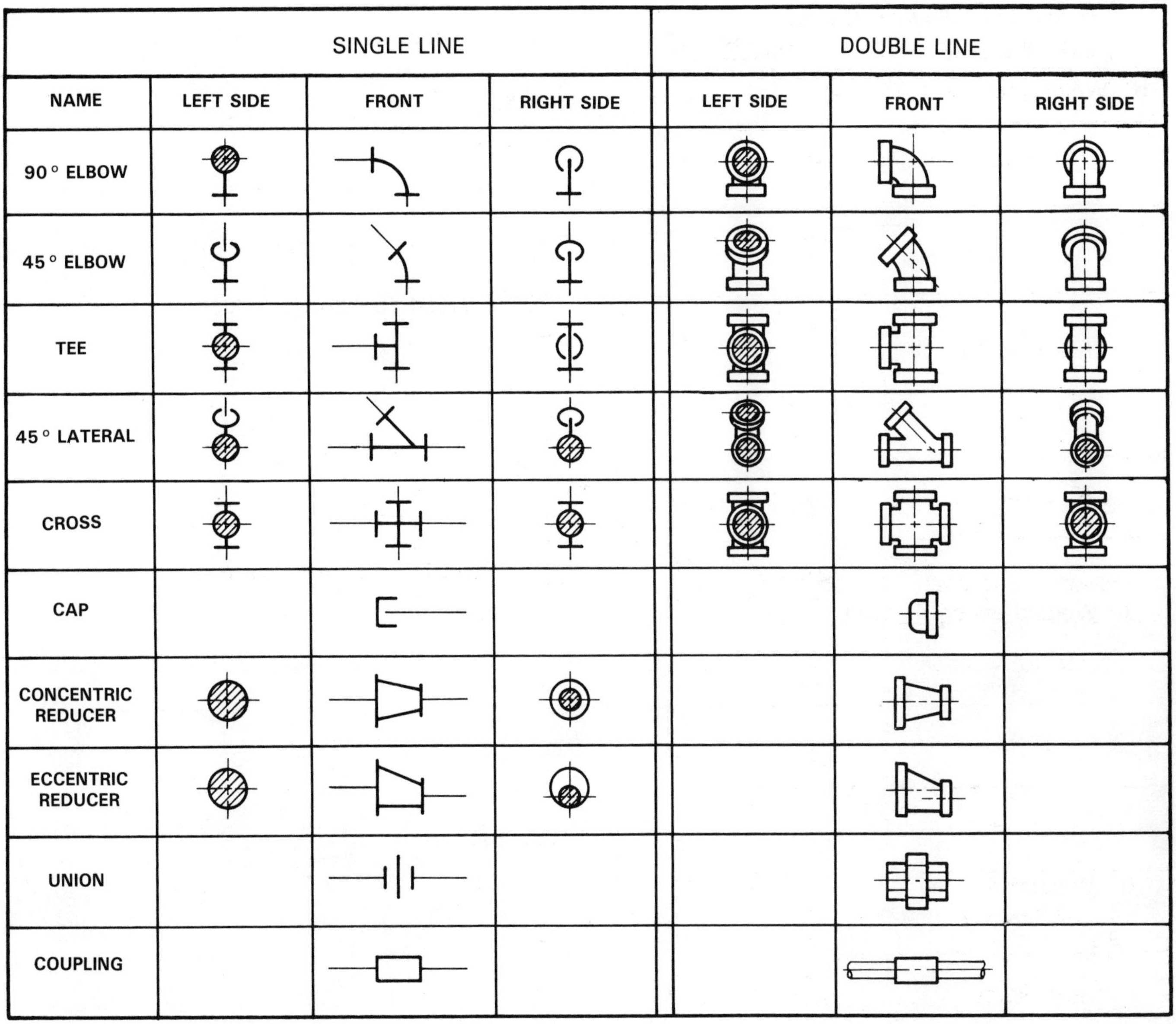

SINGLE LINE				DOUBLE LINE		
NAME	LEFT SIDE	FRONT	RIGHT SIDE	LEFT SIDE	FRONT	RIGHT SIDE
90° ELBOW						
45° ELBOW						
TEE						
45° LATERAL						
CROSS						
CAP						
CONCENTRIC REDUCER						
ECCENTRIC REDUCER						
UNION						
COUPLING						

Fig. 2-34. This chart illustrates single line and double line screwed pipe fitting symbols.

REVIEW QUESTIONS

1. Identify the following abbreviations:
   ID _____
   OD _____
   NPS _____
2. Explain the difference between buttwelded and socketwelded pipe. _____
   _____
   _____
   _____
3. A _____ is always placed between two flanges.
4. Explain briefly the pros and cons of double line and single line piping. _____
   _____
   _____
   _____
5. What are two methods of classifying pipe thickness? _____
   _____
   _____
   _____

27

Sketch the following fittings:

DOUBLE LINE   SINGLE LINE

6. Welded tee

12. Threaded tee

13. Flanged concentric reducer

7. Threaded 90° ell

14. Welded concentric reducer

8. Welded eccentric reducer

15. Stub-in

9. Welded 45° ell

16. O'let fittings are handy for producing _____ at various points in the pipe run.

10. Flanged lateral

17. How do slip-on and weld neck flanges differ?

_____
_____
_____
_____
_____
_____
_____
_____

11. Union

18. A _____ is a vertical pipe in which the fluid is flowing up.

19. A _____ is a vertical pipe in which the fluid is flowing down.

PROBLEMS

PROB. 2-1. Draw the four orthographic views of the double line fittings shown in Fig.

Prob. 2-1. Show all centerlines and section lines (where necessary).

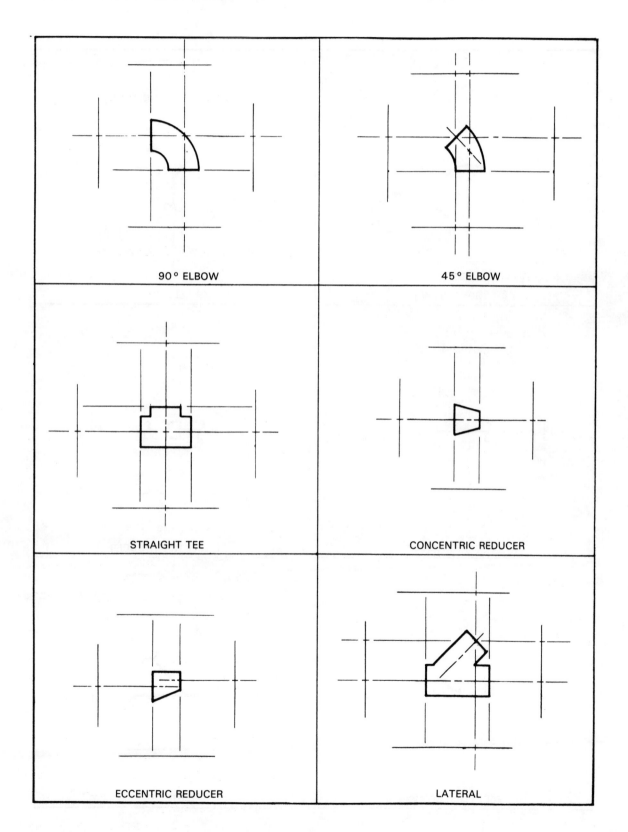

90° ELBOW

45° ELBOW

STRAIGHT TEE

CONCENTRIC REDUCER

ECCENTRIC REDUCER

LATERAL

Fig. Prob. 2-1

PROB. 2-2. Draw the four missing views of each of the single line fittings shown in Fig. Prob. 2-2.

PROB. 2-3. Visit a construction company and ask for a donation of old or defective fit-

tings. Clean and mount. Use for classroom reference.

PROB. 2-4. Write to companies in your area and ask for fitting catalogs and price lists. Use these in classroom exercises.

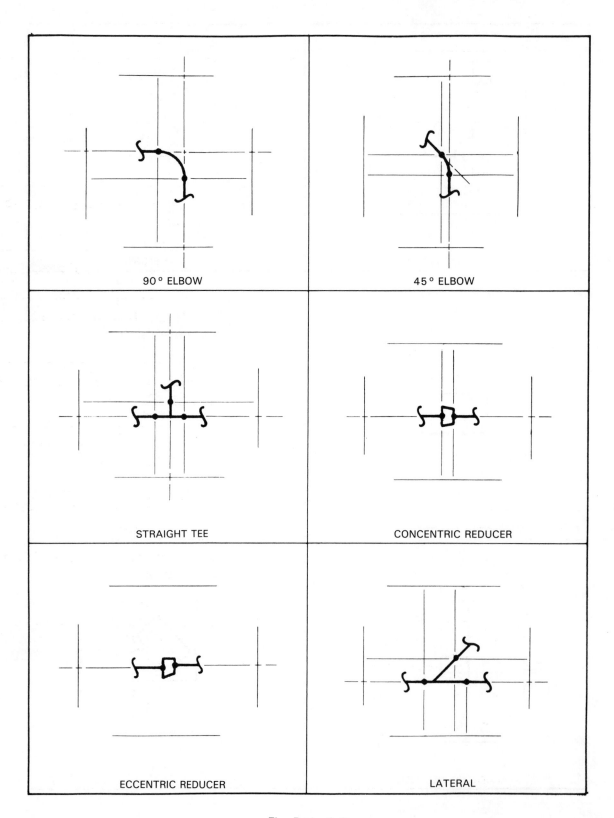

90° ELBOW

45° ELBOW

STRAIGHT TEE

CONCENTRIC REDUCER

ECCENTRIC REDUCER

LATERAL

Fig. Prob. 2-2

PROB. 2-5. Use the fitting chart in Appendix B to obtain the dimensions required in this exercise:

WELDING FITTINGS

a.   A dimension for 4 in. LR ell

_____

b.   B dimension for 8 in. 45° ell

_____

c.   D dimension for 6 in. 90° ell

_____

d.   Wall thickness of Schedule 40 8 in. pipe

_____

e.   OD of 12 in. pipe

_____

f.   E dimension of 10 in. cap

_____

g.   Wall thickness of Schedule 140 16 in. pipe

_____

h.   H dimension of 6 x 4 concentric reducer

_____

i.   C dimension of 4 x 3 straight tee

_____

j.   M dimension of 10 x 8 reducing tee

_____

k.   H dimension of 12 x 6 eccentric reducer

_____

l.   ID of 6 in. Schedule 80 pipe

_____

m.   ID of 1 1/2 in. light wall pipe

_____

n.   A dimension for 24 in. LR ell

_____

WELDING FLANGES

o.   O dimension for 4 in. 150# SO Flange

_____

p.   Y dimension for 6 in. 150# WN Flange

_____

q.   Y dimension for 16 in. 150# SO Flange

_____

r.   C dimension for 8 in. 400# WN Flange

_____

s.   B.C. of 10 in. 300# SO Flange

_____

t.   Bore of 8 in. Schedule 80 WN Flange

_____

u.   Bolt hole size of 24 in. 400# Flange

_____

v.   Number of bolt holes in 4 in. 1500# Flange

_____

w.   C dimension of 12 in. 900# BF

_____

x.   Y dimension of 18 in. 150# WN Flange

_____

PROB. 2-6. Draw the required four views of each of the pipe assemblies in Figs. Prob. 2-6A, Prob. 2-6B, Prob. 2-6C, and Prob. 2-6D.

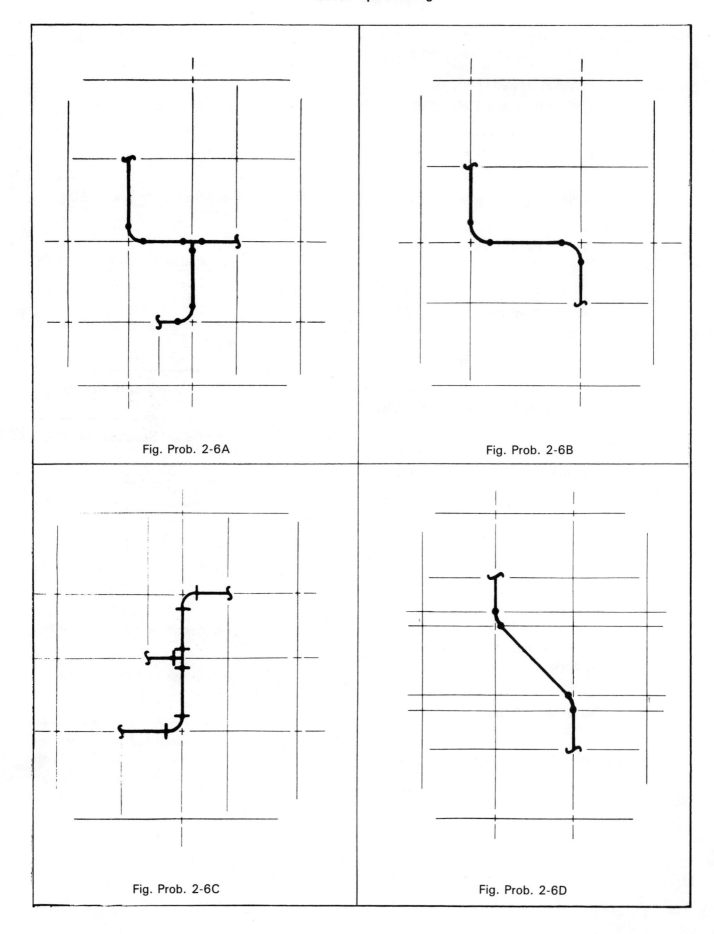

Fig. Prob. 2-6A

Fig. Prob. 2-6B

Fig. Prob. 2-6C

Fig. Prob. 2-6D

Control panel in right foreground is located at ''dry end'' of a paper machine.
(Dominion Engineering Works, Ltd.)

Operator checks instrumentation built into a control panel in a liquified natural gas plant.
(CBI Industries, Inc.)

Chapter 3

VALVES AND INSTRUMENTATION

Fluids within a piping system need to be controlled, regulated, and directed; hence the need for valves. See Fig. 3-1. Simply put, a VALVE is a gate used to control the flow of a fluid. We'll look at some variations on that gate directly, and how they are shown on piping drawings.

Within any process piping system, the fluids vary greatly with respect to temperature, pressure, volume, acidity, etc. The job of detecting and sensing these variables falls on pieces of equipment termed ''instruments.'' This chapter explores the straightforward method in which instrumentation is represented on drawings and examines several examples of their use.

Fig. 3-1. Many types of valves are used in process piping. (Crane Co.)

35

VALVES

VALVES are used to turn something on or off. They also can be adjusted to vary the rate of flow, permit flow in one direction only, switch flow along different routes, or discharge fluid from a system. Fig. 3-2 shows the basic valve symbol used on piping drawings. Variations on this theme indicate the special type of valve or the method of operation. NOTE: Fig. 3-14 illustrates the drawing symbols used to represent the basic valve types discussed in this chapter.

Fig. 3-2. Basic valve symbol is shown. Also see Fig. 3-14.

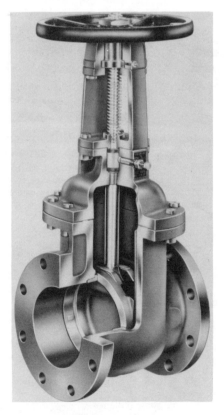

Fig. 3-3. Gate valve. (Crane Co.)

GATE VALVE: This is the most common type of valve used by plants and mills. It is designed for open or shut operation only. It is often manually controlled. A "gate" rises and falls as the handwheel

is turned. A "knife gate" version, Fig. 3-3, is available for use in areas of limited space. It costs less and is lighter in weight.

Gate valves may be operated in several ways. The most common way is by means of a handwheel.

Fig. 3-4. Chainwheel operator. (Rovang, Inc.)

Fig. 3-5. Gear operator. (Crane Co.)

If the valve is overhead out of reach, a "chain-wheel," Fig. 3-4, may be used. A handwheel "extension" can be used for gate valves located below operating level or platform level. For gate valves requiring less operating torque, "gear" operators, Fig. 3-5, are employed. A handwheel is still used, but a spur gear or bevel gear is added.

Fig. 3-7. Relief valve. (Kunkle Valve Co., Inc.)

RELIEF AND SAFETY VALVES: These valves are the insurance in a piping system. When the pressure in the pipe or vessel goes beyond a specified limit, the relief valve, Fig. 3-7, opens and releases the gas or fluid until the pressure falls below the critical point. The important part of a typical relief valve is the spring which is designed to "give" at a point termed the "set pressure." Your home hot water heater has a relief valve.

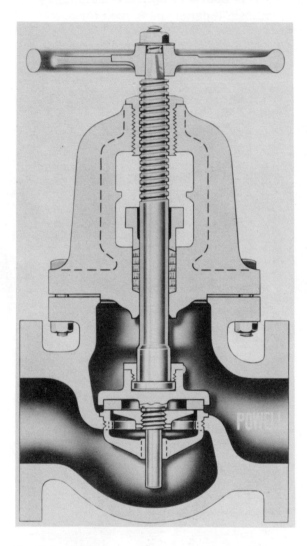

Fig. 3-6. Regulating valve. (The Wm. Powell Co.)

REGULATING (THROTTLING) VALVE: The principal function of a regulating valve, Fig. 3-6, is to regulate the flow. Faucets on your home washbasins are good examples of this valve. Liquid flowing through a regulating valve must change direction, thereby creating a flow resistance that permits closer regulation of the fluid. Regulating valves are normally considered efficient up to 6 in. in size. A few members of this family are "globe," "plug," "ball," and "needle" valves. Regulating valves are usually shown with a dot in the center of the symbol.

Fig. 3-8. Safety valve. (Kunkle Valve Co., Inc.)

Safety valves, Fig. 3-8, are a rapid-opening specimen often referred to as ''pop-off'' valves. Safety valves permit momentary full flow of steam and other gases, while relief valves release only a small volume of liquid.

Fig. 3-9. Control valve. (The Wm. Powell Co.)

CONTROL VALVE: Control valves, Fig. 3-9, do just that: control. Pressure and flow rate can be regulated by hydraulic, pneumatic, or electrically operated control valves. Some of the variables that flow valves can react to are temperature, pressure, level, and flow rate. Sensors placed within a tank or vessel, or upstream of the control valve, transmit signals to the valve. The valve responds by opening or closing according to preset limits. Control valves usually are sized smaller than line size for positive regulation and to avoid excessive wear of the seat.

BUTTERFLY VALVE: These valves are of the rotating stem type, Fig. 3-10. The flat plate (similar to that of the gate valve) rotates in place and requires only a quarter turn for opening and closing. This valve is useful in tight places because of its compactness. It can also be used for positive flow control.

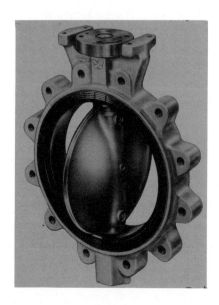

Fig. 3-10. Butterfly valve. (Crane Co.)

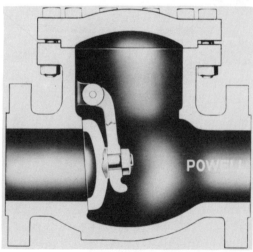

Fig. 3-11. Top and Bottom. Check valve.
(The Wm. Powell Co.)

CHECK VALVE: Flow is allowed to go in one direction only in lines that employ check valves. See Fig. 3-11. Variations of this valve are numerous,

Fig. 3-12. Flush-bottom tank valve. (The Wm. Powell Co.)

but the basic principle still applies. The pipe becomes a one-way street.

FLUSH-BOTTOM TANK VALVE: This is usually a globe type valve located at the low point of a tank to facilitate easy discharge of fluids, slurries, etc. Note the unique shape of this valve in Fig. 3-12.

Fig. 3-13. Steam trap. (Armstrong Machine Works)

TRAP: This is an automatic valve that collects air, water, and gases in steam lines and discharges

them without releasing steam. See Fig. 3-13. It is also used in air lines to trap water. Note the symbol used for this valve in Fig. 3-14.

INSTRUMENTS

The dashboard of your automobile houses several instruments similar to those used in industry. One instrument measures the rate of movement, another reads the oil pressure, and still another indicates the temperature of the coolant. All of these variables and more must be monitored in modern industrial processes, and it must be done quickly and accurately.

INSTRUMENT FUNCTIONS

Instruments are seldom, if ever, shown on piping drawings. However, instrument functions are always indicated within a symbol. Often the pipe drafter will show only the connection fitting for the instrument (usually a coupling or half coupling), and then the symbol containing the function. See Fig. 3-15.

The majority of instruments are of four basic types: flow, level, pressure, and temperature. The jobs they perform are few even though they may be used for a variety of purposes.

The basic functions of instruments are:
1. To *sense* one of the process variables, usually flow rate, level, pressure, or temperature.
2. To *transmit* the measurement of a variable from the instrument to a secondary location, such as a control panel.
3. To *indicate* the measurement of a variable. This can occur at the control panel or at the instrument by means of paper roll and pen, digital display, or dial indicator. Flashing lights and alarms are also means of indicating critical levels or points.
4. To *record* the measurement.
5. To *control* the variable. A valve is most often used to perform this final function.

PROCESS VARIABLES

A ''variable'' is a characteristic of a fluid under certain conditions. Temperature and pressure are two common variables, and these are measured by instrumentation. There are others, but they are best shown in a standard established by the Instrument Society of America. It is known as ISA standard S5.1 and is shown in Fig. 3-16. This coding is used internationally although most companies alter it somewhat to fit their requirements. Therefore, become familiar with your company standards before drawing or labeling instruments.

VALVE SYMBOLS		
TYPE	FLOW DIAGRAM	PIPING DRAWING (FLANGED)
GATE		
REGULATING (BALL) (GLOBE)		
CHECK		
BUTTERFLY		
RELIEF	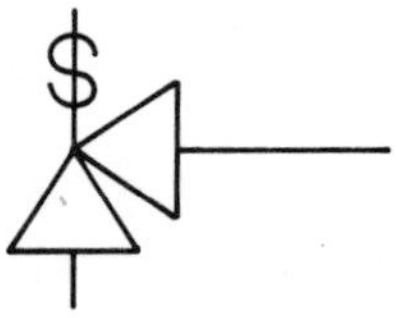	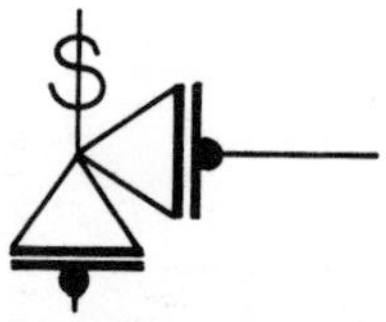
CONTROL	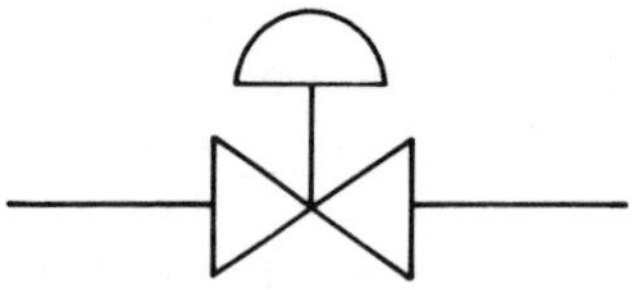	
FLUSH BOTTOM		
TRAP		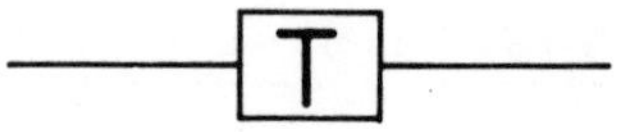

Fig. 3-14. Chart shows valve symbols used on flow diagrams and piping drawings.

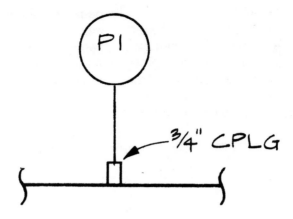

Fig. 3-15. Instrument symbol and connection fitting are illustrated.

INSTRUMENT IDENTIFICATION TABLE (ISA S5.1 CODING)			
UPPER CASE LETTER	**FIRST LETTER** process variable	**SECOND LETTER** type of reading or function	**THIRD LETTER** additional function
A		ALARM	ALARM
C	CONDUCTIVITY	CONTROL	CONTROL
D	DENSITY		DIFFERENTIAL
E		ELEMENT	
F	FLOW		RATIO
G		GLASS	
H	HAND		HIGH
I	CURRENT (electric)	INDICATING	
L	LEVEL		LOW
M	MOISTURE		INTERMEDIATE
* O		ORIFICE	
P	PRESSURE		
R		RECORDER	
S	SPEED	SAFETY	SAFETY
T	TEMPERATURE	TRANSMITTER	
V	VISCOSITY	VALVE	VALVE
W	WEIGHT	WELL	
* X		TRANSMITTER	
*Not a part of the original ISA S5.1. Optional usage.			

Fig. 3-16. Instrument identification table is based on Instrument Society of America standard.

INSTRUMENT REPRESENTATION

As stated earlier, instruments are seldom, if ever, shown on a piping drawing. A symbol is used and a connection fitting may be shown on the piping. The symbol used is a circle, and it appears the same on flow diagrams and piping drawings. Figs. 3-17 through 3-22 offer a few examples of the ap-

pearance of instruments on flow diagrams and piping drawings. Note that the instrument itself is the same on both. Take some time to study these examples and become familiar with the more commonly used instruments and how they are applied.

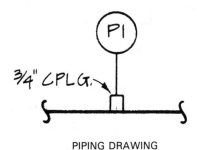

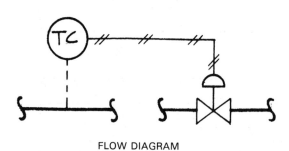

Fig. 3-17. Pressure indicator.

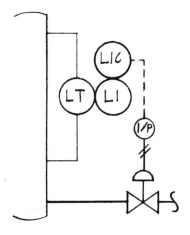

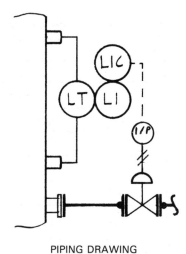

Fig. 3-19. Level indicating controller.

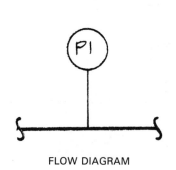

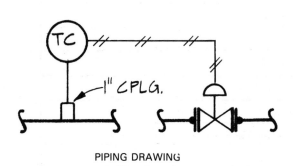

Fig. 3-18. Temperature controller.

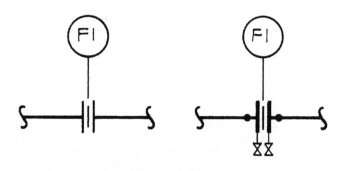

Fig. 3-20. Flow indicator.

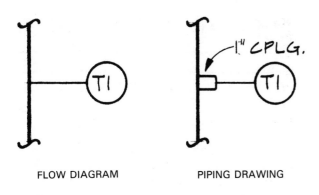

FLOW DIAGRAM   PIPING DRAWING

Fig. 3-21. Temperature indicator.

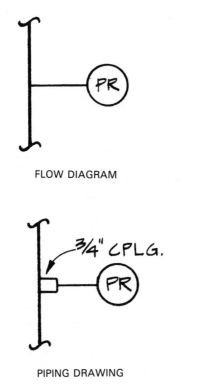

FLOW DIAGRAM

PIPING DRAWING

Fig. 3-22. Pressure recorder.

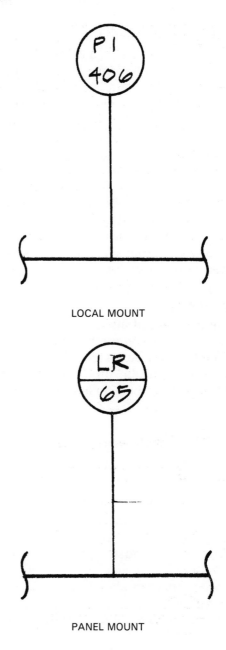

LOCAL MOUNT

PANEL MOUNT

Fig. 3-23. Instrument mounting symbols.

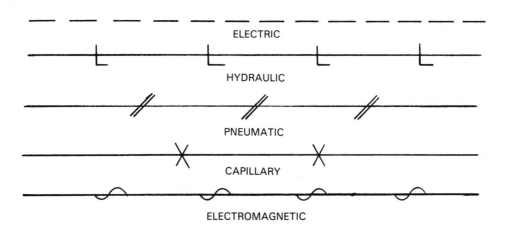

ELECTRIC

HYDRAULIC

PNEUMATIC

CAPILLARY

ELECTROMAGNETIC

Fig. 3-24. Instrument signal leads.

The instrument symbol is composed of three parts. The symbol itself is a circle. The circle may be open, indicating a locally mounted instrument, or it may have a horizontal line through it, representing panel mounting. See Fig. 3-23. A pressure gage mounted on the pipe would be local mounting and a pressure gage in an instrument panel of a control room would be panel mounting.

The second part of the symbol is the instrument identification, Fig. 3-23. This is the information obtained from ISA S5.1. The third part is the instrument "loop number." A LOOP is an interconnected group of instruments. Many instrument loops are found in any industrial system, and each one must be tagged with a number.

SIGNAL LEADS

The final aspect of instrument identification we need to discuss is the method of operation. How is each instrument activated? Some are operated by electrical impulses, others by pneumatics. A complete list of symbols for instrument signal leads is shown in Fig. 3-24.

REVIEW QUESTIONS

1. Name three functions of valves:
   a. _____
   b. _____
   c. _____
2. What is the most common valve used in industry? _____
3. A valve located above reach is operated by means of a _____ .
4. Sketch the symbol for a globe valve.

5. What is the difference between relief and safety valves? _____
   _____
   _____
6. Sketch the symbol for the type of valve that allows flow in one direction only.

7. What are the uses of a trap? _____
   _____
   _____

8. What are the four basic types of instruments?
   a. _____
   b. _____
   c. _____
   d. _____
9. What is process variable? _____
   _____
   _____
10. What is most often used to control a process variable? _____
    _____
11. Sketch the difference between a panel and local mounted instrument.

12. What is a loop? _____
    _____
13. On which two drawings will instruments be found?
    a. _____
    b. _____
14. Sketch and label the symbols for four types of instrument signal leads.

   a.   b.

   c.   d.

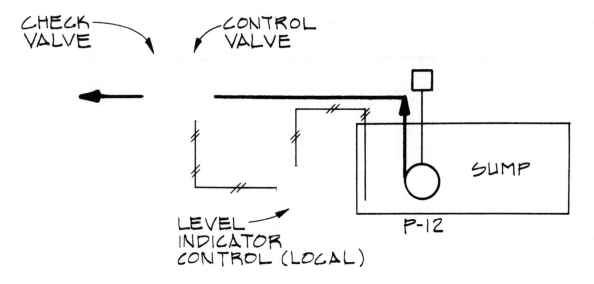

Fig. Prob. 3-1A

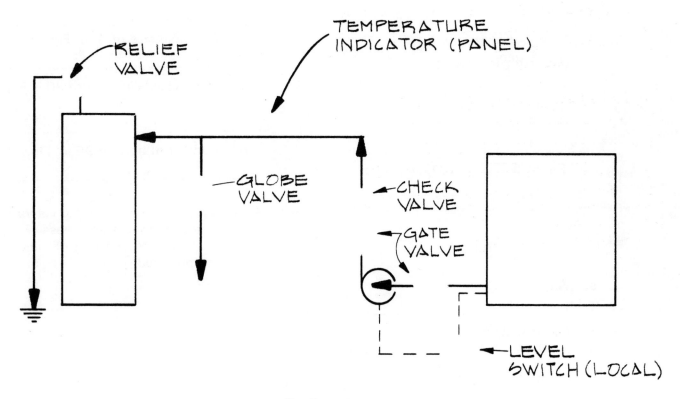

Fig. Prob. 3-1B

PROBLEMS

PROB. 3-1. Figs. Prob. 3-1A and Prob. 3-1B are portions of a flow diagram with missing valves and instruments. Sketch in the correct valves and instruments as indicated in the notes.

PROB. 3-2. Fig. Prob. 3-2 gives verbal descriptions of five different instruments and shows their connection points on a pipe. Sketch the instrument symbol for each, letter the correct designation and loop number, and indicate whether it is local or panel mounted.

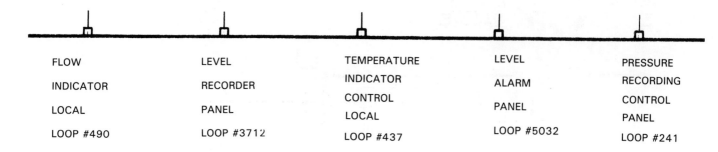

FLOW	LEVEL	TEMPERATURE	LEVEL	PRESSURE
INDICATOR	RECORDER	INDICATOR	ALARM	RECORDING
LOCAL	PANEL	CONTROL	PANEL	CONTROL
		LOCAL		PANEL
LOOP #490	LOOP #3712	LOOP #437	LOOP #5032	LOOP #241

Fig. Prob. 3-2

PROB. 3-3. Use the manufacturer's valve specifications in Appendix C to find the required dimensions in this exercise.

JENKINS

a. F-F of 4 in. Fig. 2325 gate

_____

b. Flange diameter of 2 1/2 in. Fig. 1325 gate

_____

c. Center to spindle top of 8 in. Fig. 2325 gate

_____

d. F-F of 6 in. Fig. 1317-A globe

_____

CRANE

e. Weight of 10 in. #461 gate

_____

f. F-F of 5 in. #465 gate

_____

g. Center to top of 20 in. #464 1/2 OS & Y gate

_____

h. Weight of 3 in. #372

_____

i. End to end of 2 1/2 in. #373

_____

j. Center to top of 14 in. #383

_____

FABRI-VALVE

k. B.C. of 16 in. Fig. 45

_____

l. Weight of 48 in. Fig. 134

_____

m. F-F of 16 in. Fig. 71

_____

n. Bolt hole size of 8 in. Fig. 11

_____

o. Handwheel diameter of 20 in Fig. 78

_____

p. Number of bolts in 96 in. Fig. 50

_____

PROB. 3-4. Draw the four orthographic views of the pipe and fitting assemblies in Figs. Prob. 3-4A and Prob. 3-4B in the spaces provided.

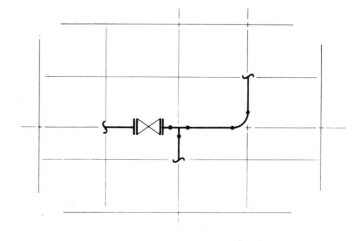

Fig. Prob. 3-4A

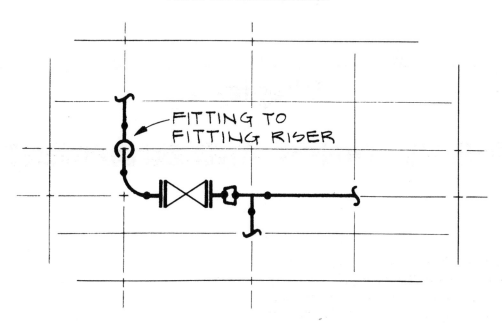

Fig. Prob. 3-4B

PROB. 3-5. Contact companies in your local area that supply valves and ask for brochures, catalogs, and price lists. Use this information in classroom exercises.

PROB. 3-6. Obtain photographs of all types of valves and make a wall chart. Group valves according to basic types. Show a cutaway view of each type and several examples around each cutaway.

PROB. 3-7. Convert the isometric in Fig. Prob. 3-7 to a single line and double line drawing in the spaces provided. Your view should be in the direction the arrow is pointing.

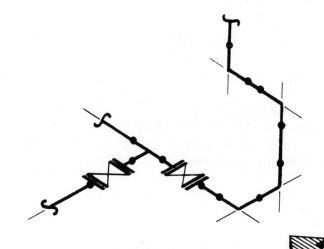

Fig. Prob. 3-7

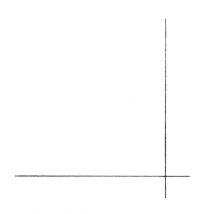

SINGLE LINE

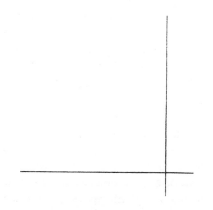

DOUBLE LINE

Chapter 4

PUMPS, TANKS, AND EQUIPMENT

Pipe drafting does not deal exclusively with the drawing of pipes. The pipes must have an origin and a termination point. Usually, these origins and terminus points are pieces of equipment. Pumps and tanks, for example, are the most common things that pipes connect. However, there also exists a wide range of equipment that must be drawn or "piped" by the drafter.

PUMPS

PUMPS are the workhorses of any process plant, and the centrifugal pump is the type most frequently used. This pump operates at a constant rate and will supply a steady flow of fluid for the process. Pumps are the most common pieces of equipment in the plant, and they are represented simply on process pipe drawings. Familiarize yourself with the methods of representation because you will be drawing many of them.

GENERAL ARRANGEMENT SYMBOL

The GENERAL ARRANGEMENT is one of the first drawings that is completed. It is basically a background drawing, and equipment shown on a general arrangement is usually depicted by simple symbols. A centerline is often all that will be drawn. This is normally the case with pumps. However, the pump pad or foundation should show, as well as the pump centerline. Fig. 4-1 illustrates a common method used on general arrangements. Note that the pump has been labeled and dimensions have been given from the nearest steel columns.

Most pumps should be drawn in the manner shown in Fig. 4-1. However, some pumps and their motors may be quite large and, therefore, an outline of the equipment should be drawn. This outline, Fig. 4-2, may serve as a reference for clearances on future drawings.

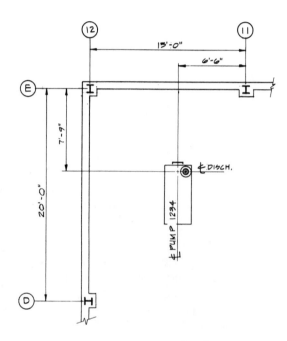

Fig. 4-1. General arrangement drawing features a simple pump symbol.

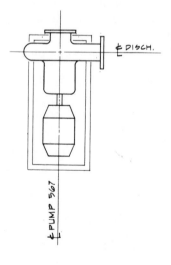

Fig. 4-2. A large pump is outlined on a general arrangement.

FLOW DIAGRAM SYMBOLS

SYMBOLS are simple graphic representations of the real thing, and nowhere are pumps shown more simply than on flow diagrams. Some companies prefer to use a circle as the symbol. Others embellish the circle with various projections and bases. None the less, the circle is the basis for the flow diagram pump symbol, Fig. 4-3. Company standards vary on the size of the pump symbol, but the range is normally from 3/8 in. to 3/4 in. in diameter.

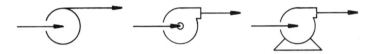

Fig. 4-3. A sampling of pump symbols is presented.

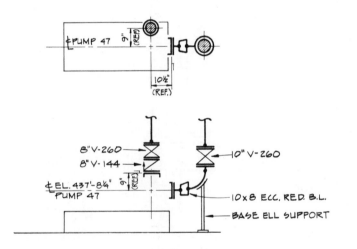

Fig. 4-4. Plan view and elevation view of a centrifugal pump are shown.

PIPING DRAWING SYMBOL

PIPING DRAWINGS contain all the details of the piping system. The pump representation on this type of drawing is a bit more involved than on previous ones. Piping drawings are composed of plans, sections, and details. Fig. 4-4 shows an example of a plan and elevation of a typical centrifugal pump.

The CENTERLINE of the pump is the most important line on the plan view. Crossing the axis of the pump is the discharge centerline. The centerline of pump and motor is always dimensioned. See Fig. 4-4. Note that the suction and/or discharge flanges must be dimensioned from the pump centerline if

they show as an edge view. These dimensions are from a pump dimension sheet and are normally labeled as reference or ''ref.''

The elevation view shows the axis centerline, and it is labeled with both the pump number and its elevation. The elevation is the pump centerline height off the floor. Note again the reference dimension given to the discharge flange in Fig. 4-4.

GASKET SYMBOL

The little symbol that represents a gasket is shown in Fig. 4-5. This L-shaped symbol rests on

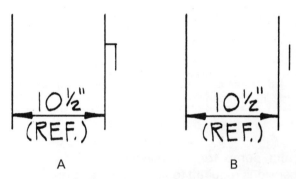

Fig. 4-5. Gasket symbols: A — L-shaped symbol projects from right extension line. B — Another gasket symbol parallels extension line.

the extension line of the flange, and it indicates if the gasket is included in the dimension or omitted. The example at A in Fig. 4-5 informs us that the gasket is *not* included in the dimension. Remember to draw this little symbol because the thickness of the gasket may make a difference when calculating dimensions and lengths of pipe and fittings. The example at B in Fig. 4-5 shows another form of the gasket symbol.

ISOMETRIC PUMP SYMBOL

Pumps drawn in isometric should be shown with most, if not all, of the information given on the piping drawings. Fig. 4-6 is an isometric drawing of the pump shown in Fig. 4-4. Note that the pump is labeled, dimensioned, and has a centerline elevation.

VENDOR PUMP DATA

Line drawings of two variations of the centrifugal pump are shown at A and B in Fig. 4-7. The drafter must be able to use vendors' catalogs to find the

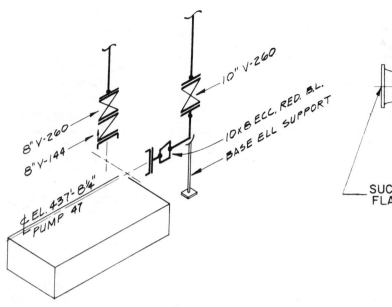

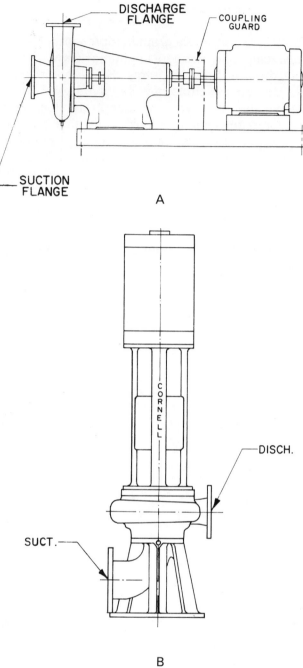

Fig. 4-6. Isometric pump symbol on piping drawing contains full information for connection into piping system.

correct pump for the given application, and the dimensions required to draw it. For example, dimensions relating to the height of the pump centerline and the location of the flange faces are frequently used. Therefore, it often is the responsibility of the drafter to locate these dimensions in brochures or catalogs provided by the pump manufacturer or vendor. Fig. 4-8 is an example of the type of information provided.

TANKS

TANKS are containers that come in a great variety of shapes and sizes. They are used to store almost everything. Tanks are not difficult to draw, but often the attachments and embellishments are detailed. Let's take a look at some characteristics of these ponderous pieces of equipment.

SHAPES AND STYLES

Tanks can be built to any specifications that the client requires: square, cylindrical, or spherical. They can be erected vertically, horizontally, or at an angle. Some basic tank shapes are shown in Fig. 4-9.

FLOW DIAGRAM TANK SYMBOLS

The shapes drawn in Fig. 4-9 are used to depict tanks on flow diagrams. Also see Fig. 4-10. The basic shape is shown, and inlet and outlet pipes are joined to the tank. No tank details are given on the

Fig. 4-7. Centrifugal pumps are commonly used in process plants. A — Horizontal centrifugal pump. B — Vertical centrifugal pump. (Cornell Pump Company)

flow diagram unless specifically required. These details usually are reserved for the piping drawings and tank drawings.

PIPING DRAWINGS

A more detailed view of the tank is shown on the piping drawing. All pipes connected to the tank are drawn, as are the manholes, ladders, and platforms.

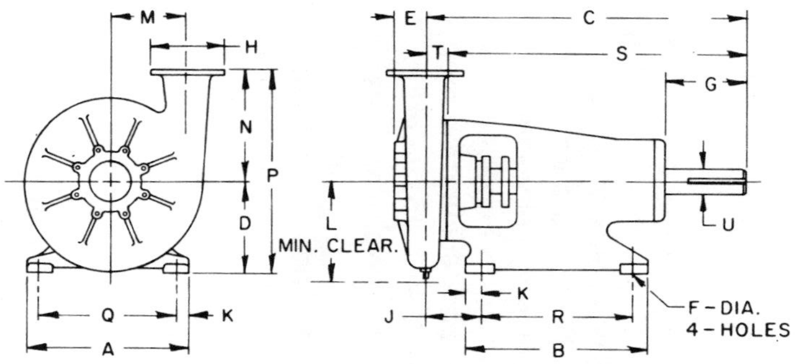

FIGURE 1

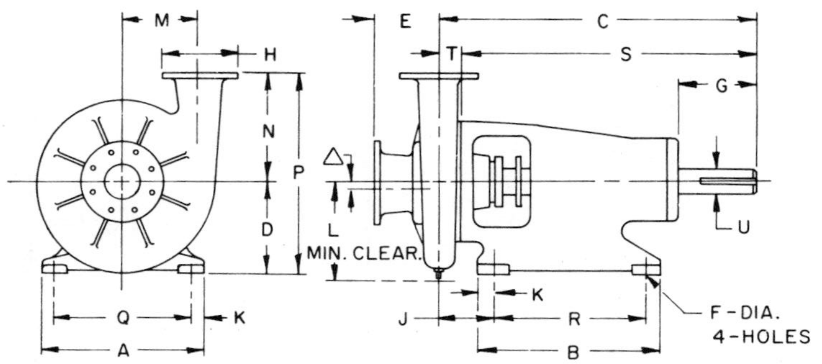

FIGURE 2

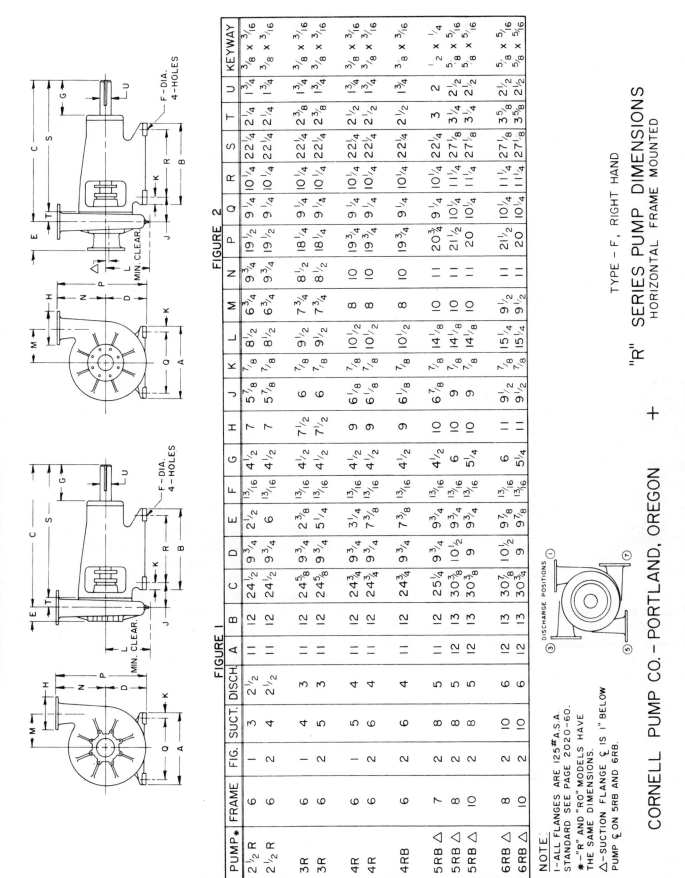

PUMP*	FRAME	FIG.	SUCT.	DISCH.	A	B	C	D	E	F	G	H	J	K	L	M	N	P	Q	R	S	T	U	KEYWAY
2 1/2 R	6	1	3	2 1/2	11	12	24 1/2	9 3/4	2 1/2	13/16	4 1/2	7	5 7/8	7/8	8 1/2	6 3/4	9 3/4	19 1/2	9 1/4	10 1/4	22 1/4	2 1/4	1 3/4	3/8 x 3/16
2 1/2 R	6	2	4	2 1/2	11	12	24 1/2	9 3/4	6	13/16	4 1/2	7	5 7/8	7/8	8 1/2	6 3/4	9 3/4	19 1/2	9 1/4	10 1/4	22 1/4	2 1/4	1 3/4	3/8 x 3/16
3R	6	1	4	3	11	12	24 5/8	9 3/4	2 3/8	13/16	4 1/2	7 1/2	6	7/8	9 1/2	7 3/4	8 1/2	18 1/4	9 1/4	10 1/4	22 1/4	2 3/8	1 3/4	3/8 x 3/16
3R	6	2	5	3	11	12	24 5/8	9 3/4	5 1/4	13/16	4 1/2	7 1/2	6	7/8	9 1/2	7 3/4	8 1/2	18 1/4	9 1/4	10 1/4	22 1/4	2 3/8	1 3/4	3/8 x 3/16
4R	6	1	5	4	11	12	24 3/4	9 3/4	3 1/4	13/16	4 1/2	9	6 1/8	7/8	10 1/2	8	10	19 3/4	9 1/4	10 1/4	22 1/4	2 1/2	1 3/4	3/8 x 3/16
4R	6	2	6	4	11	12	24 3/4	9 3/4	7 3/8	13/16	4 1/2	9	6 1/8	7/8	10 1/2	8	10	19 3/4	9 1/4	10 1/4	22 1/4	2 1/2	1 3/4	3/8 x 3/16
4RB	6	2	6	4	11	12	24 3/4	9 3/4	7 3/8	13/16	4 1/2	9	6 1/8	7/8	10 1/2	8	10	19 3/4	9 1/4	10 1/4	22 1/4	2 1/2	1 3/4	3/8 x 3/16
5RB △	7	2	8	5	11	12	25 1/4	9 3/4	9 3/4	13/16	4 1/2	10	6 7/8	7/8	14 1/8	10	11	20 3/4	9 1/4	10 1/4	22 1/4	3	2	1/2 x 1/4
5RB △	8	2	8	5	12	13	30 3/8	10 1/2	9 3/4	13/16	6	10	9	7/8	14 1/8	10	11	21 1/2	10 1/4	11 1/4	27 1/8	3 1/4	2 1/2	5/8 x 5/16
5RB △	10	2	8	5	12	13	30 3/8	9	9 3/4	13/16	5 1/4	10	9	7/8	14 1/8	10	11	20	10 1/4	11 1/4	27 1/8	3 1/4	2 1/2	5/8 x 5/16
6RB △	8	2	10	6	12	13	30 7/8	10 1/2	9 7/8	13/16	6	11	9 1/2	7/8	15 1/4	9 1/2	11	21 1/2	10 1/4	11 1/4	27 1/8	3 5/8	2 1/2	5/8 x 5/16
6RB △	10	2	10	6	12	13	30 3/4	9	9 7/8	13/16	5 1/4	11	9 1/2	7/8	15 1/4	9 1/2	11	20	10 1/4	11 1/4	27 1/8	3 5/8	2 1/2	5/8 x 5/16

NOTE:

1-ALL FLANGES ARE 125# A.S.A. STANDARD SEE PAGE 2020-60.

*-"R" AND "RO" MODELS HAVE THE SAME DIMENSIONS.

△-SUCTION FLANGE ℄ IS 1" BELOW PUMP ℄ ON 5RB AND 6RB.

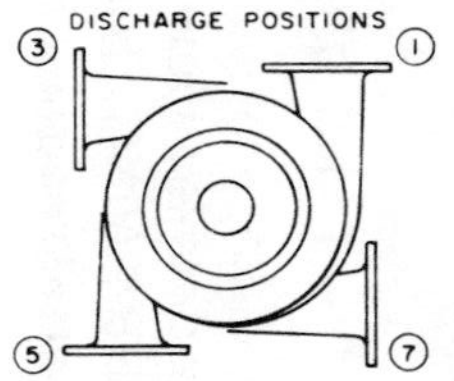

TYPE - F, RIGHT HAND

CORNELL PUMP CO. - PORTLAND, OREGON

"R" SERIES PUMP DIMENSIONS

HORIZONTAL FRAME MOUNTED

Fig. 4-8. Coded drawings and chart make up pump dimension sheet. (Cornell Pump Company)

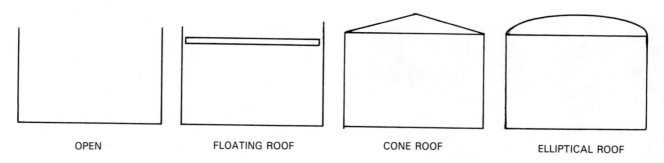

OPEN　　　　FLOATING ROOF　　　　CONE ROOF　　　　ELLIPTICAL ROOF

Fig. 4-9. These basic tank shapes are used in process pipe drafting.

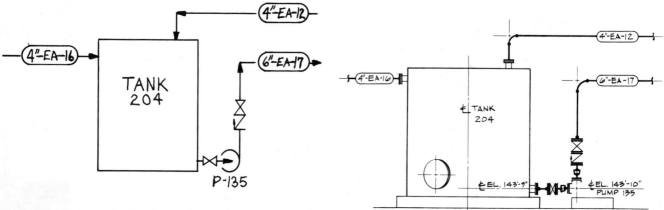

Fig. 4-10. Tank symbol is shown in use in a typical flow diagram.

Fig. 4-11. Tank symbol is more detailed in this piping elevation.

Fig. 4-11 shows how a tank is represented on a piping drawing. Note, however, that the basic shape is the same as on the flow diagram in Fig. 4-10.

TANK DRAWINGS

The most detailed view of the tank is shown on the TANK DRAWING. This drawing is created by the drafter after the tank has been designed. Complete in every detail, the drawing is sent to the tank fabricator who builds the tank and ships it to the construction site. If the tank is too large to ship, it is built at the site or shipped there in parts and assembled.

DRAWING DETAILS

The tank drawing normally does not rely on any other drawing for reference information. You might consider it an assembly drawing. All construction details are shown as are all the materials used to build it. Welding symbols may appear on the drawing, so you need to be familiar with them. Study the drawing in Fig. 4-12 and try to pick out the details as we discuss them.

Some other items shown on a tank drawing are NOZZLES and MANHOLES. Nozzles are important because they are the points at which pipes are connected. When drawing nozzles, it is important that you measure correctly and give accurate dimensions. Fig. 4-13 is an example of a nozzle projection chart used as a reference for piping drafter.

Miscellaneous features such as instrument connections, bracing, lifting eyes and hooks, davits, ladders, and cages may also appear on the tank drawing.

BILL OF MATERIAL

The BILL OF MATERIAL is a table that normally appears on the right side of the drawing. Basically it is a shopping list for the tank. All materials needed for construction of the tank are shown on the ''B.O.M.'' A minimum of four columns is needed in this table. The first is the ''item'' number, or identifying mark. This number is shown on the drawing and points to the part. The other three columns are ''size,'' ''description,'' and ''quantity.'' Some companies may add a column for material specifica-

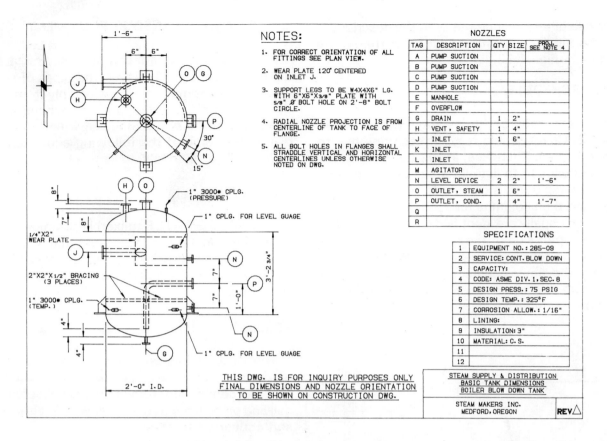

Fig. 4-12. Tank drawing provides full details of tank construction. Note nozzle schedule at right. (Sandwell International, Inc.)

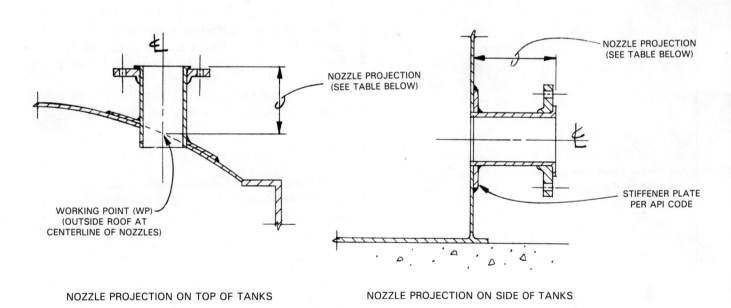

NOZZLE PROJECTION ON TOP OF TANKS

NOZZLE PROJECTION ON SIDE OF TANKS

NOTE: Unless otherwise noted on drawing, nozzles to be fabricated from standard weight ASTM A53 Gr. A pipe, and 150 lb. raised face ASTM 181 Gr. 2, ASA B16.5 slip-on flanges, bolt holes to straddle centerlines.

SIZE	1 1/2"	2"	3"	4"	6"	8"	10"	12"	14"	16"	18"	20"
PROJECTION	6"	6"	7"	7"	8"	8"	9"	9"	10"	10"	11"	11"

NOZZLE PROJECTION (UNLESS NOTED ON DRAWINGS)

Fig. 4-13. Tank nozzle projection chart lists nozzle sizes and amount of projection.

tion, while others include this with the description. Note the similar information given in the nozzle schedule in Fig. 4-12.

NOZZLE SCHEDULE

Some tanks may be "brimming" with nozzles, Fig. 4-12. Chaos would result if each one had to be dimensioned. Therefore, a NOZZLE SCHEDULE is often employed to list all the necessary dimensions. This table has a column for the NPS of the nozzle, and then columns for each dimension. The dimensions usually are identified by a letter located along the top or side of the table. A typical nozzle may be illustrated on the drawing by the letter code in place of the dimension numbers. Drawings using a nozzle schedule are shown in Figs. 4-12 and 4-14. Note letter code at left.

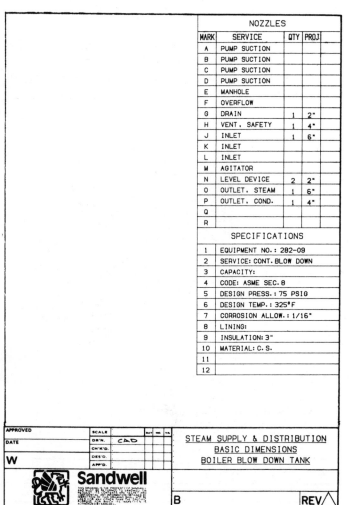

Fig. 4-14. Tank drawing nozzle schedule uses a letter code instead of dimensioning nozzles.
(Sandwell International, Inc.)

MISCELLANEOUS EQUIPMENT

Pumps and tanks are common to almost all industrial processes. However, the types of specialized equipment may vary considerably from one industry to another. Petroleum, petrochemical, pulp and paper, food processing, brewing, and power plants use some of the following equipment. See Chapter 5 for symbols.

AGITATOR

This little AGITATOR (mixer) is common to many industries and it is used to do just that: mix. It may be permanently attached to a tank or it can be portable. Basically it is a propeller attached to a shaft and motor.

BOILER

The BOILER basically is a heater fired by oil, natural gas, or even wood chips. Condensate (water that has condensed from steam) is collected in the mill and piped back to the boiler where it is reheated and converted to steam.

CLARIFIER

The CLARIFIER is a large, open tank into which wastewater and effluent is piped or drained. The bottom of the clarifier is sloped to the center, and a rake slowly scrapes the settled material to the center where it is pumped off. The "clear" or clarified liquid flows off the top, over a weir (dam). Then it is piped elsewhere for further treatment.

COLUMN

A FRACTIONATION COLUMN is common to the petroleum industry. It is used to distill various products. Basically it is a still. A preheated feed, in this case crude oil, is fed into the column. Several products can be distilled from the crude as it rises through the column, and these are termed "fractions" or "cuts." A few of the common distillates are heating oil, gasoline, fuel gases, naptha, and paraffin.

CONDENSER

The CONDENSER is a piece of equipment that does exactly what its name implies: it condenses. Gases enter one side and are cooled by cold water or a refrigerator. This causes the gases to condense and exit the other side as a liquid.

COMPRESSOR

Just as a pump increases the pressure of a liquid, a COMPRESSOR increases the pressure of a gas or vapor. A low-pressure vapor enters the compressor, it is compressed, then discharged at a higher pressure.

CYCLONE

The motion inside the CYCLONE (piece of separation equipment) is similar to a storm. Solids and/or gases enter the cyclone at an angle that creates a whirling, circular motion inside. The heavier materials fall to the bottom and lighter materials exit at the top. The pulp and paper and the wood products industries make extensive use of cyclones.

DRYER

The DRYER (rotary kiln) is a long, slightly inclined, large diameter tube used to dry substances, notably lime, in the pulp and paper industry. The wet material recovered from the process enters one end, slowly slides along the rotating kiln, where it is dried by a gas burner. The lime is reclaimed and reused. Fig. 4-15 pictures a rotary sludge kiln in operation at a paper company.

EVAPORATOR

The EVAPORATOR (concentrator) used in the pulp and paper industry is similar in function to a condenser, but the process is reversed. Water is removed or evaporated from a liquid chemical compound through steam heating. The liquid eventually becomes concentrated and can then be reused within the process or sold.

FILTER

The FILTER (rotary drum) separates solids from liquids by means of a vacuum on the drum. Solids adhere to a perforated belt on the rotating drum due to the vacuum inside. As the drum rotates, a scraper removes the solids or "cake" from the belt. A conveyor may be used to remove the cake. Meanwhile, the liquid within the filter is piped elsewhere for further treatment.

REFINER

REFINERS are high-speed grinders used in the food processing and pulp and paper industries. See Fig. 4-16. Coarse material is fed between two grinding plates spinning rapidly in opposite directions, and a fine material is discharged from the refiner.

Fig. 4-15. Rotary lime sludge kiln is used in drying operations. (Fuller Company, Bethlehem, PA)

Fig. 4-16. Refiners at a paper mill grind coarse material into fine particles. (Beloit Corporation)

VESSEL

A VESSEL is a tank with "innards." Something is usually happening within a vessel, whereas the liquid within a tank just sits there. The activity inside a vessel may be a chemical reaction (reactor), separation, distillation, or accumulation.

EQUIPMENT STANDARDS

Keep in mind that all companies possess standards that specify all of the drawing conventions and techniques to be used by the drafter. Most firms illustrate equipment with fairly universal symbols, but there always are exceptions. Therefore, whenever you are drawing a new piece of equipment, always look to the standards for the correct symbol or drawing method.

REVIEW QUESTIONS

1. Sketch the pump symbol for each of the following types of drawings:

FLOW DIAGRAM   ISOMETRIC   PIPING PLAN

2. Why are centrifugal pumps the most popular for use in industrial process systems? _____

_____

_____

3. What is the difference between a tank and a vessel? _____

_____

_____ .

4. Sketch three common tank shapes used on flow diagrams.

5. What is the purpose of the tank drawing, and who will use it? _____

_____

_____ .

6. The piece of equipment that allows solids to settle out of wastewater is a _____

_____ .

7. What is a "fraction," and what piece of equipment produces it? _____

_____ .

8. The drafter must often obtain pump data from what sources? _____

_____ .

9. What information is found on the Bill of Material? _____

_____

_____ .

10. Briefly compare and contrast pumps and compressors. _____

_____

_____

_____

_____ .

11. What piece of equipment is used to mix a substance within a tank? _____

_____

_____ .

PROBLEMS

PROB. 4-1. Redraw the plan view shown in Fig. 4-1, using the scale of 3/8" = 1' - 0" on B size vellum. Use the pump shown in Fig. 4-4.

PROB. 4-2. Draw a plan view of Fig. 4-11. Locate the pump discharge on the pump centerline. Locate line 4" - EA - 12 off center 1' - 0" from the centerline of the pump. Use B size vellum.

PROB. 4-3. Draw the following pieces of equipment on a sheet of B size vellum:
   a. Column
   b. Rotary kiln
   c. Blower
   d. Cyclone
   e. Bucket conveyor
   f. Clarifier

PROB. 4-4. Fig. Prob. 4-4 illustrates a portion of a flow diagram containing a tank and a pump. All of the valves and fittings have been omitted except for the weld neck flanges attached to the pump. Notes are given to indicate the type of fittings and valves that should be placed in the diagram. Sketch the indicated valves and fittings in the spaces provided. Use the vendors' catalog pages reproduced in the appendix to find the type of valves shown. Draw a double line nozzle on the tank.

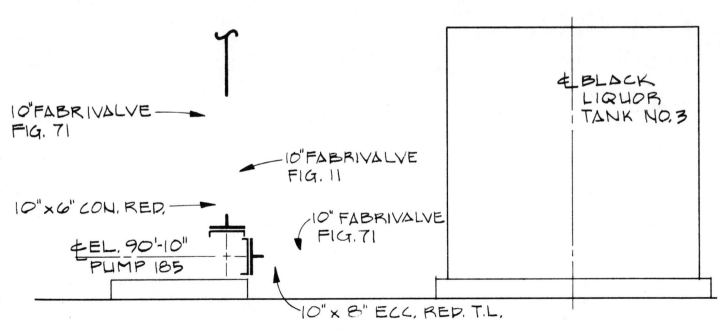

Fig. Prob. 4-4

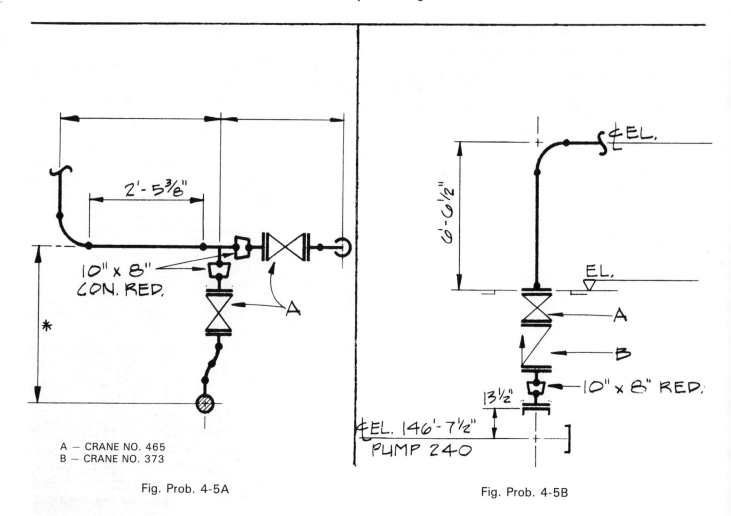

2'-5³⁄₈"

10" x 8"
CON. RED.

A

*

A — CRANE NO. 465
B — CRANE NO. 373

Fig. Prob. 4-5A

₵EL.

6'-6½"

EL.

A

B

10" x 8" RED.

13½"

₵EL. 146'-7½"
PUMP 240

Fig. Prob. 4-5B

Label the centerline elevation of the nozzle in the sketch.

PROB. 4-5. Calculate the needed dimensions and elevations in drawings A and B in Fig. Prob. 4-5. Gaskets are 1/16 in. thick.

All flanges are 150#. The dimension with the asterisk involves trigonometric calculations (refer to Chapter 8, which discusses this type of calculation in detail).

Chapter 5

FLOW DIAGRAMS

The schematic representation of the flow of fluids through a system is called a FLOW DIAGRAM. Symbols are used to represent equipment, and the drawing has no scale. Flow diagrams enable nontechnical persons to comprehend the basic functions of complicated systems. They may be used as just a preliminary drawing of a system, or they may contain all the necessary facts from which to construct process piping drawings.

Companies will vary on their use of flow diagrams and the details they include on them. Some will use a flow diagram that contains pipe specifications, valves, instrumentation, and all of the equipment for the system. Others will create a simple flow diagram showing equipment, flow lines, a few valves, instruments, and some temperatures, pressures, and flow line volumes. In addition to this basic flow diagram, these companies will create what is termed a ''P & I'' diagram. This ''piping and instrumentation'' diagram is the detailed version of the flow diagram.

For our discussion of the techniques used to create these drawings, we'll use the term ''flow diagram.'' Keep in mind that each company will have its variations of this type of drawing, but the information presented here will always apply. So let's study the flow diagram and see how it's put together.

FUNCTION OF THE FLOW DIAGRAM

Flow diagrams are generally one of the first drawings done of a new system or an addition to an existing system. *But why are they created in the first place? What is their function?*

SYSTEM IDENTIFICATION

The physical system that supports an industrial process begins as thoughts and ideas in someone's head. Those are transferred to paper or chalkboards

Fig. 5-1. A flow diagram begins as ideas are sketched on a chalkboard. (CBI Industries, Inc.)

in the form of sketches, Fig. 5-1, and verbal descriptions. The person responsible usually is an engineer or technician/designer. Once the ideas begin to jell, the engineer may request that a drafter convert the sketches to a flow diagram. When this is accomplished, the system is there for the world to see . . . and change.

The system, hence the flow diagram, will be altered and revised many times after it is put on paper. This is an integral part of the design process discussed in Chapter 1, and something every student in this field should realize. The system, as it appears on the flow diagram, can be toyed with, engineered, designed . . . and seen. The project engineer will approve or disapprove; the client will present his or her views; and the flow diagram becomes the vehicle for feedback, discussion, and revisions. See Fig. 5-2.

Fig. 5-2. Engineers use flow diagrams to revise aspects of a system's design before completion of the project. (Courtesy CH2M HILL)

PIPING DRAWING REFERENCE

Information given on the flow diagram is used to design the piping plans and elevations. This is one of the most important functions of the flow diagram. The drafter must be able to pick symbols, numbers, and sizes off the flow diagram and apply them to the construction of piping drawings.

The ability to use a flow diagram to construct a piping drawing is not something expected of a junior drafter. This is an ability that is picked up through a learning process on the job. Once a drafter is able to do this with accuracy and completeness, he or she becomes an extremely valuable asset to the company. The first step in achieving that goal is to understand the workings of a flow diagram. Let's begin.

EQUIPMENT

The flow diagram is a schematic-type drawing and, therefore, relies on symbols to represent actual pieces of equipment. Symbols are a stylized representation of the real thing and are created with two things in mind: simplicity and ease of interpretation. The equipment symbols that are used on flow diagrams adhere to these two requirements. A simple, basic outline portrays the shape of the equipment and decreases drawing time.

TYPES AND SHAPES

Each company possess its own set of drawing standards for EQUIPMENT SHAPES. However, there are many equipment symbols that are common within certain industries. Basic shapes seldom change, but company "A" may prefer to add a bit more detail to a symbol that company "B." Refer to Fig. 5-3 for a sampling of some flow diagram equipment symbols. There are no universal sizes to draw the equipment. Drawing layout, company standards, and client preference will determine that.

There is one important point to remember when laying out a flow diagram. Equipment sizes *should* appear in proportion to one another. The example shown in Fig. 5-4 is indicative of good symbol sizes.

EQUIPMENT LABELING

LABELING should always be done last if you are drawing manually. You will avoid smudging and excess erasing if you have to move symbols or rearrange your layout. When you do label, it should be done with care and forethought. Indiscriminate labeling of equipment can result in a less-than-pleasing appearance on your drawing.

The best location to place a label is within the symbol, slightly above center. See symbol A in Fig. 5-5. This may not be possible if there are other details within the symbol. The illustrations in Fig. 5-5 indicate the preferred labeling sequence, with A being the first choice. The placement of labels also depends on the amount of space available.

EQUIPMENT NUMBERS

Each piece of equipment is assigned a number, chosen by the engineering firm or by the client. The EQUIPMENT NUMBERS are always placed on the flow diagram with the label. See Fig. 5-4. The drafter must be certain that these numbers appear on the flow diagram. They will be used when constructing the piping drawings and will also appear on equipment schedules.

FLOW LINES

Two types of FLOW LINES exist: primary and secondary. These lines indicate major and minor flows. Major flows may be all lines above 14 in. in diameter, but this will vary from one company to another. Size not considered, the major or primary flow is always the main run of pipe.

LINE CROSSINGS AND CONNECTIONS

Major flow lines are thick and command attention on a flow diagram. Other flow lines and instrumentation signal lines may cross major flows, but they are always broken at the crossing. When

Flow Diagrams

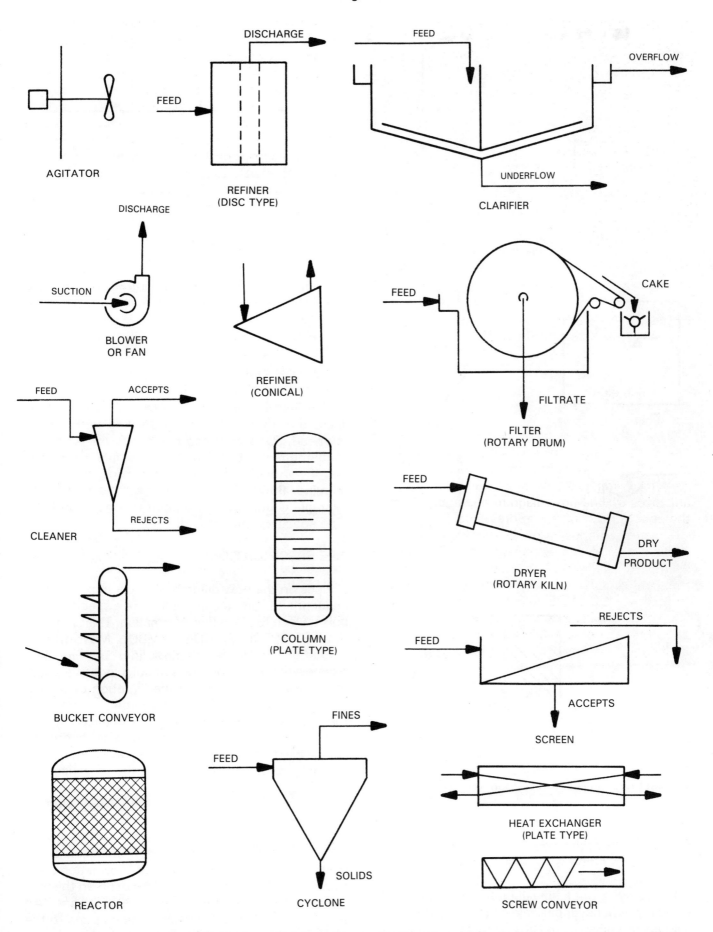

Fig. 5-3. Some typical flow diagram equipment symbols are shown.

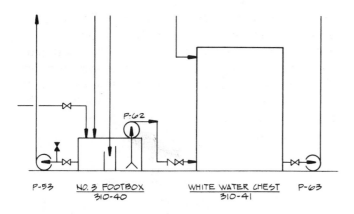

Fig. 5-4. Proportional equipment sizes are evident on this flow diagram.

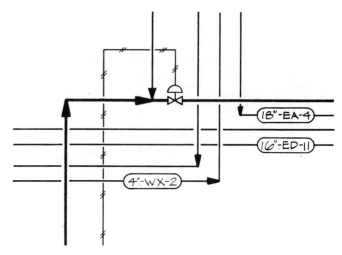

Fig. 5-6. This flow diagram presents a good example of correct line weights and proper flow line crossings and junctions.

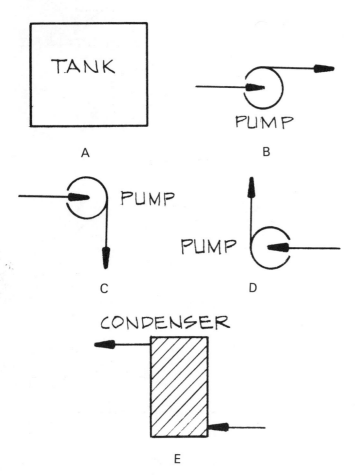

Fig. 5-5. Proper location of equipment labels is illustrated. Best location is within symbol, as shown at A.

two flow lines of the same size meet at right angles, a common method is to break the horizontal line, Fig. 5-6.

When laying out a flow diagram, *try* to avoid line crossings whenever possible. Unfortunately, this is seldom possible.

FLOW LINE DIRECTION

The direction of flow must be indicated on flow lines, and the best way to do it is with an arrowhead. *But where and in what form?* A variety of methods exist. In Fig. 5-7, example A requires that the arrows on major flows be larger than those on minor flows. Example B has same-size arrows. Example C utilizes only a point on one end of the pipe specification symbol.

PIPE SPECIFICATIONS

Pipes on the flow diagram, like equipment, must be identified. Some companies use a specific symbol in which to place this information. This is termed the PIPE SPECIFICATION SYMBOL. Most often it is located directly in the flow line. See Fig. 5-7. Example C shows how the symbol may serve a second purpose of indicating the direction of flow.

The amount and type of information given within the pipe "spec" symbol will vary with the company. Basic information such as the pipe size, contents, and an identification number are always shown. The example in Fig. 5-8 reveals that the pipe size is 6 in. in diameter. The "WM" is a code established by the engineering firm or the industry to identify the contents of the pipe. The number "124" is a tag number given to identify that specific pipe.

The drafter uses this information when constructing the piping drawings. Specific information as to the type of pipe and fittings to be used on this line (WM) is found in the project specifications. An engineer or designer normally assigns sizes to the pipe, but it is up to the drafter to indicate the cor-

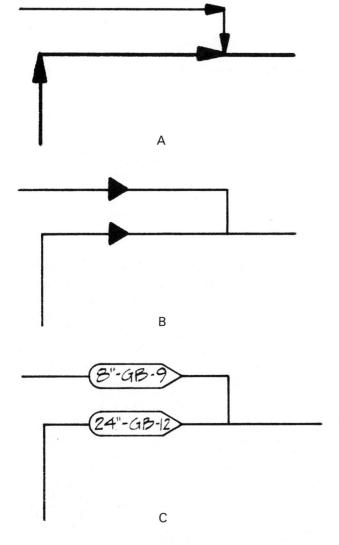

DRAIN SYMBOLS is given in Fig. 5-9. The symbols represent discharge into either the atmosphere or a sewer. Atmospheric vents are most often found on the tops of tanks, but they can occur in a pipe run. Discharge to sewer may be located anywhere along a flow line, but the most common location is at the bottom of tanks and after pumps.

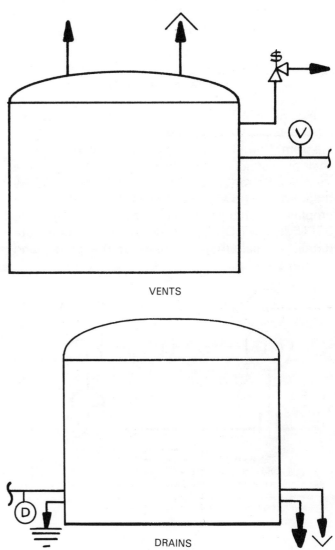

VENTS

DRAINS

Fig. 5-7. Methods of indicating flow: A — Larger arrows for larger pipe. B — Same size arrows. C — Point on end of pipe specification symbol.

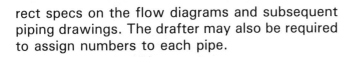

Fig. 5-8. This pipe specification symbol gives pipe size, contents, and identification number.

Fig. 5-9. Vent and drain symbols indicate where system vents to atmosphere and drains to a sewer.

rect specs on the flow diagrams and subsequent piping drawings. The drafter may also be required to assign numbers to each pipe.

VENTS AND SEWERS

Flow lines often end abruptly at any number of small symbols. A sampling of these VENT and

VALVE SYMBOLS

The shape of the basic valve symbol is much like that of a bow tie. Variations of this symbol identify a specific type of valve. See Fig. 5-10. Use of the correct valve symbol on the flow diagram is important because the drafter must use this information when creating the piping plans.

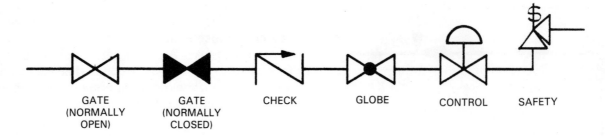

Fig. 5-10. These are common valve symbols shown on flow diagrams. Note method used to identify valves that are normally closed.

INSTRUMENT SYMBOLS

INSTRUMENTATION is a vital aspect of any industrial process, and it must be shown on the flow diagram. Companies using just the flow diagram as their only schematic of the system show *all* of the instrumentaiton. Other firms may use the flow diagram to show the basics of the system, and employ another drawing, the PIPING AND INSTRUMENTATION DIAGRAM, to give the complete details (in schematic format) of the piping and instrumentation.

INSTRUMENT TYPES

In Chapter 3 we discussed in detail the classifications of instruments and their functions. Now let's briefly examine the appearance of the basic types of instruments on flow diagrams. There are four types: temperature, pressure, flow, and level. Fig. 5-11 provides examples of each type of instrument, and brief descriptions of each are given. Also see Fig. 3-19 for instrument signal leads.

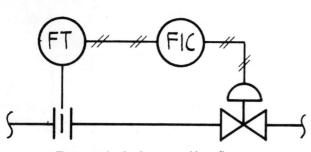

The control valve is operated by a flow indicating controller (FIC) which receives a pneumatic signal from the flow transmitter. The transmitter is attached to a flow orifice which measures flow.

A

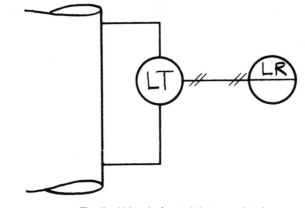

The liquid level of a tank is transmitted to a panel mounted level recorder (LR) which makes a continuous record of the level.

B

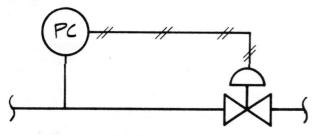

Pressure controller (PC) senses pipe pressure and, via a pneumatic transmitter, operates the control valve. Pressure within the pipe or vessel is then regulated.

C

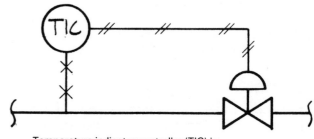

Temperature indicator controller (TIC) is an indicator and control valve combined to regulate temperature. Capillary tube connects TIC to pipe.

D

Fig. 5-11. Four instruments are shown in place in flow diagrams. A — Flow transmitter/flow indicating controller. B — Level transmitter/level recorder. C — Pressure controller. D — Temperature indicator controller.

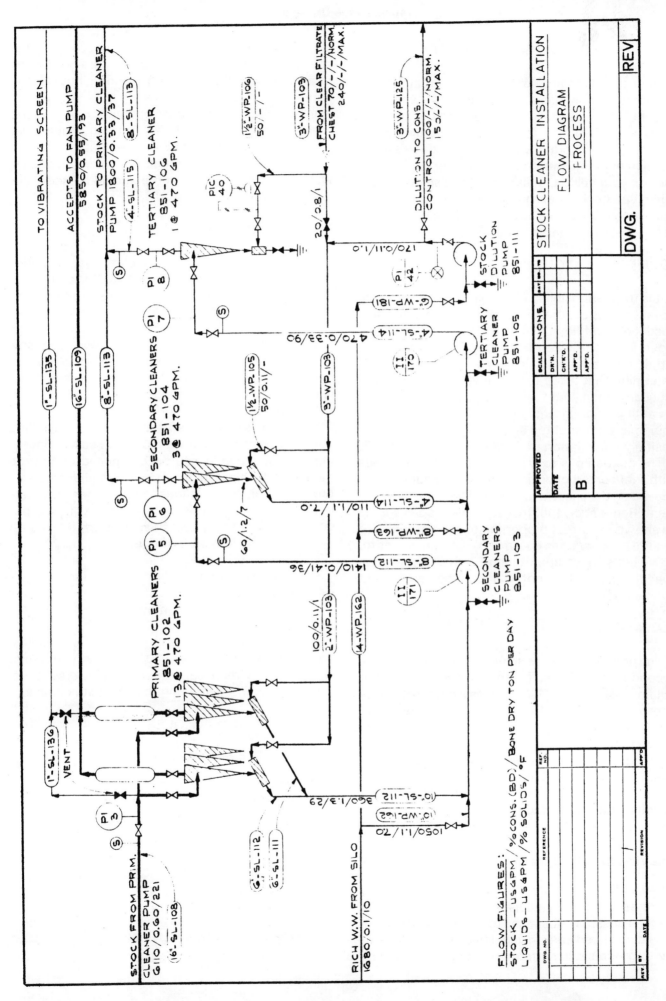

Fig. 5-12. Industrial print serves as an example of a good flow diagram layout. (Sandwell International, Inc.)

FLOW DIAGRAM LAYOUT

Flow diagrams are not difficult to create if you adhere to some basic procedures. A well constructed flow diagram can be a pleasure to work with, but a hastily made, ill-conceived drawing can be confusing. Therefore, it's a good idea to sketch a preliminary equipment layout before putting any lines on your vellum, mylar, or video display screen. When you begin your manual drafting layout, your lines should be drawn with a light blue, non-photo pencil or a hard lead such as 6H.

EQUIPMENT LAYOUT

It is the responsibility of the pipe drafter to create a practical layout of the equipment with some sort of continuity of flow. The flow of the process should move from one side of the drawing to the other, rather than zigzagging or jumping around. If you determine that more than one level of equipment is needed, then your first guidelines would be those indicating the ground levels of the equipment. Equipment not situated at ground level can then be positioned in relation to the ground line, Fig. 5-12.

The next step is to draw the equipment outlines with light construction lines. Size of the outlines will depend on the space available and the type of equipment. Remember, too, that equipment sizes should be shown in correct proportion to each other. Also be sure to allow open space between equipment for flow lines, instrumentation, valves, and line specifications. Do not darken the equipment outlines yet.

FLOW LINES

The primary flow lines should be drawn next, then secondary flow lines. Try to group lines together, but no closer than 1/4 in. It gives a neat, organized appearance and also keeps long lines in one or two areas of the drawing. This is shown clearly in Fig. 5-13.

Avoid line crossings and direction changes as much as possible. The fewer the turns and interferences, the easier it will be to interpret the drawing. Carefully study the two examples of the same flow diagram in Fig. 5-13.

VALVES, INSTRUMENTATION, AND LINE SPECS

VALVES, INSTRUMENTATION, and LINE SPECS are three types of symbols that will appear within the flow lines. The locations of these symbols need to be considered early in your initial diagram layout. Try to group similar information together if possible. This is called "information grouping." Line specification symbols, for example, are good ones to arrange together. Fig. 5-11 shows how this is done.

Valves and instruments do *not* have to be grouped together, nor should they be. But you should take the time to locate them in the approximate positions in which they will reside. For example, valves that will be located near the pump should be shown in that position on the flow diagram.

THE FINISHED DRAWING

Once your initial layout is complete, you can darken your lines. Begin at the top of the drawing and work down. Draw all of your lines, then go back and do the lettering. This, too, should be done from top to bottom. Always keep a sheet of clean paper under your hands as you letter, avoiding any smudges. Any crosshatching or shading that is needed should always be done last. The less there is on the drawing to smudge, the fewer smudges there will be.

If you are using a computer aided drafting system, you may want to employ a technique called "layering." Your drawing can be composed of two or more layers. One layer might be the equipment symbols, another the flow lines, and another the labeling. The following is a list of layers that you possibly could use to construct a flow diagram.

1. Major equipment symbols.
2. Pumps and valves.
3. Instrumentation.
4. Flow lines.
5. Line specification symbols.
6. Labeling.

When you use the layering technique, it allows you to work with only the information you need. Hence, the screen can remain uncluttered even though your entire drawing may be quite complex.

REVIEW QUESTIONS

1. What is a flow diagram? _____
_____ .

2. What is one of the most important uses of a flow diagram? _____
_____
_____ .

3. What should appear inside the equipment symbol on a flow diagram? _____
_____ .

4. What are the two types of flow lines? ____
_____ .

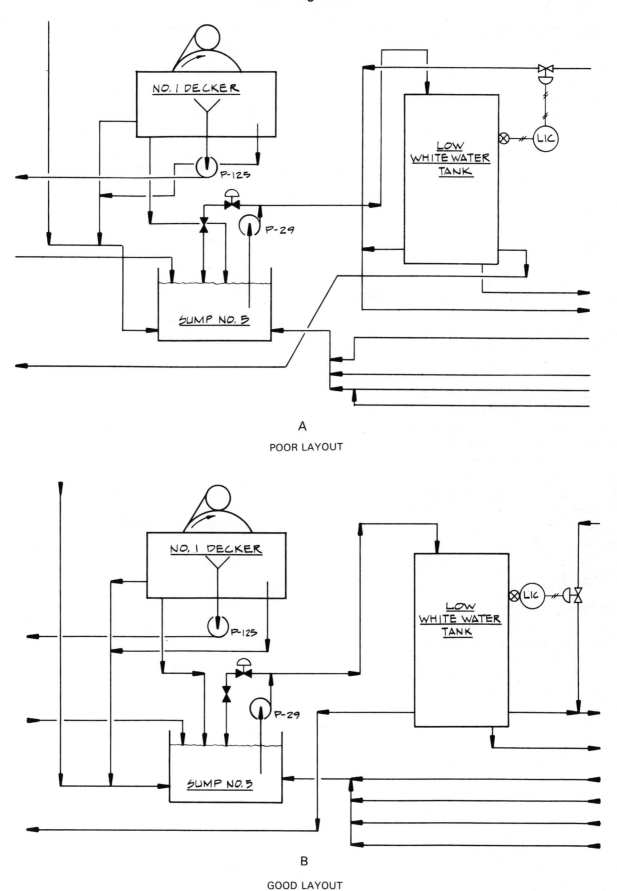

A

POOR LAYOUT

B

GOOD LAYOUT

Fig. 5-13. Flow lines on a flow diagram should present a neat, organized appearance. A — This poor layout has too many turns and line crossings. B — This good layout of same elements has better routing and grouping of flow lines.

5. Why is the pipe specification so important?

_____

_____

6. Sketch the following valve symbols:

8. Briefly describe a good flow diagram layout sequence. _____

_____

_____

_____ .

9. How are normally closed valves represented?

_____

10. Sketch two examples of vents and sewers.

GLOBE

RELIEF

A

CHECK

B

VENTS

GATE

CONTROL

7. Sketch the following signal leads:

C

ELECTRIC

CAPILLARY

D

SEWERS

11. Which drawing gives complete details of the piping system in schematic format? _____

_____

PNEUMATIC

HYDRAULIC

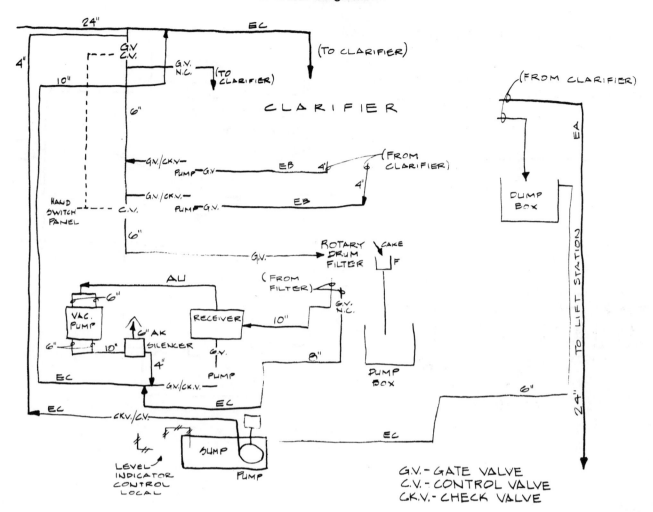

Fig. Prob. 5-2

PROBLEMS

PROB. 5-1. Choose any process, sequence of occurrences, or steps of production you can think of and create a flow diagram for it. This can be a freehand sketch with emphasis on creativity and layout.

PROB. 5-2. Fig. Prob. 5-2 is a rough sketch of a flow diagram. Much of the equipment, valves, and instruments has been omitted. Redraw this flow diagram on a separate sheet of C size vellum and insert the proper symbols for the missing equipment. Notes in parenthesis are for your information only, do not put these on the drawing. Place line specifications in each pipe. Sizes and spaces are shown. Don't forget flow arrows. Lines above 14 in. diameter are major flows. Pumps should be 3/8 in. diameter and instruments 7/16 in. diameter. Draw equipment in some degree of proportion. In actual installa-

tion, clarifier is 200 ft. in diameter, drum filter is approximately 6 ft. in diameter, so be certain the filter is the smaller symbol.

PROB. 5-3. Fig. Prob. 5-3 shows a *poor* flow diagram layout sketch. In the space provided, neatly sketch a new layout, using the suggestions mentioned in this chapter. Redraw the sketch on a B size sheet of vellum.

PROB. 5-4. Instructor: Obtain blueprints of flow diagrams from local companies. Assign different segments of the prints to students and have them redraw the segment with emphasis on improving the layout and presentation of data.

PROB. 5-5. Create a flow diagram of the water and sewer system in your home. Boxes and rectangles can be used for the various fixtures. Pipe fittings need not be shown but indicate all valves, appliances, and use points.

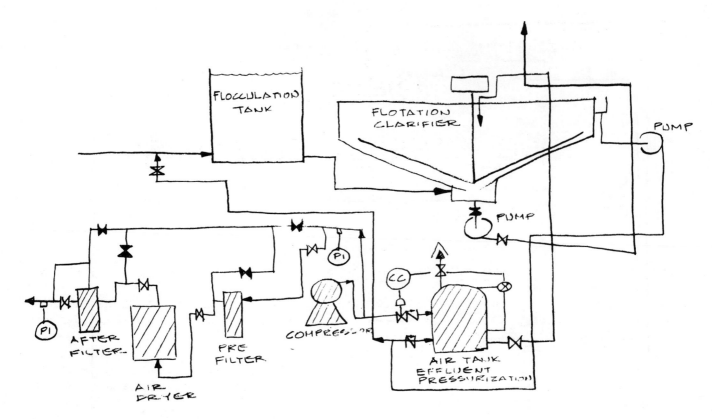

Fig. Prob. 5-3

Space provided for student drawing.

Chapter 6

PIPING PLANS AND ELEVATIONS

The piping drafter "wades into deeper water" when beginning the piping plans and elevations. These drawings contain all the information necessary to construct the system. Flow diagrams, P & I diagrams, structural drawings, and vendor information must all be used to obtain the information necessary to create the piping plans and elevations. These drawings are the true representatives of process piping drafting. Let's examine how they are drawn.

PIPING PLANS

The PIPING PLANS are important drawings that represent a large investment of time once they are completed. The best approach is to "be prepared" before putting any lines on the drawing paper. To construct the piping plans, you must use flow diagrams, vendor information, structural drawings, tank drawings, equipment schedules, project specifications, and possibly site plans and general arrangements. Know where all this information is located before you begin.

EQUIPMENT LAYOUT

First, determine the amount of space on the paper that will be used for the equipment layout drawing. Define your limits. Decide upon a scale, if you haven't already. Next, locate and draw the centerlines of the principal piece or pieces of equipment that will show on the plan. The location of the equipment on the drawing will be determined by the area of the mill you're working with and the coordinates of the match lines you are using (if any).

MATCH LINES are used when another drawing is done of the area adjacent to the one you're working on. Match lines may be needed on more than one side depending on the size of the area being drawn. Some plans do not need match lines. Once the main pieces of equipment have been located,

you can locate all remaining equipment with centerlines.

Your next task is to draw in the outlines of the equipment you just located. Any nozzles, platforms, concrete pads, or foundations that will show should be drawn at this time. If the equipment is inside a building, then the walls and structural steel columns should be drawn. The first stages of a layout are shown in Fig. 6-1.

At this point, you will have used tank and equipment drawings, structural drawings, site plans, and general arrangements for references.

PIPING LAYOUT

The flow diagram or P & I diagram comes into play when you work on the piping layout. You must know the size and type of pipe that runs between equipment. This information is found on the flow diagram. An experienced pipe drafter is responsible for routing the pipes without assistance, but the junior drafter often works from sketches or preliminary drawings done by the group leader, an engineer, or a designer.

Draw the pipe centerlines lightly. If an area will be congested with pipe, sketch both plans and elevations first to check for clearances. Fig. 6-2 shows the addition of pipes to our plan view.

If you encounter difficulty in visualizing the turns and run of the piping, begin by laying out one or more of the sections you plan to draw. This will give you another dimension, or viewpoint, to work with when drawing the plan view.

PIPE BREAKS

Important features of a piping system are often hidden below, or behind, pipes on plan and elevation views. The best way to show the hidden features is to "break" the pipe. PIPE BREAKS are

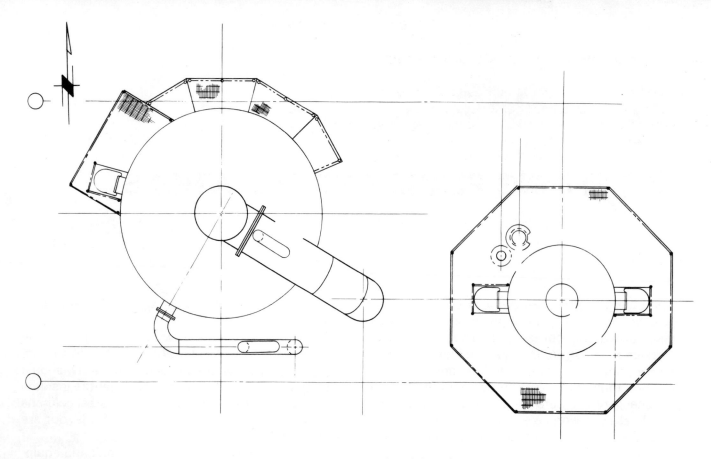

Fig. 6-1. Initial layout of a piping plan.

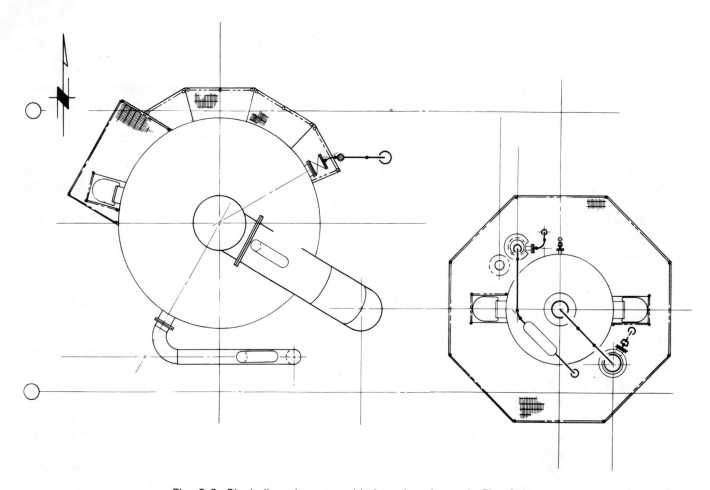

Fig. 6-2. Single line pipes are added to plan shown in Fig. 6-1.

used often and should be understood by the beginning pipe drafter.

Pipe breaks become most confusing when dealing with a stack of pipes that must be broken for identification purposes or to reveal details below. Example A in Fig. 6-3 shows a stack of pipes without breaks. Example B illustrates that same stack in the elevation view. Example C shows the plan view of the stack in single line piping with breaks applied.

Try to identify all of the pipes in example C in Fig. 6-3.

Well, how did you do? Look at example C again. Note that where two pipes meet, the break symbol is shown on the highest pipe. At the point where a pipe disappears below another, there is a small gap on the lower pipe. When a lower pipe disappears under a higher one, there is no pipe break symbol on the low pipe. *Which pipe in Fig. 6-4 is the nearest to you?*

Remember, where pipes intersect, the one that is closest to the viewer should have the break symbol because it has been broken to show hidden detail below. *Which pipe is the farthest from you in Fig. 6-5?*

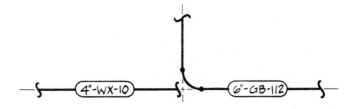

Fig. 6-4. Which pipe is closest to you?

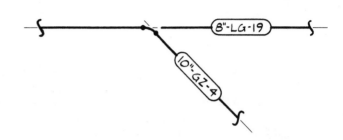

Fig. 6-5. Which pipe is farthest from you?

DIMENSIONING

One of the most important aspects of the piping plan is the dimensions. These must be accurate because they will be used later to create the piping isometrics and spool drawings. Equipment center-lines should be located from reference points such as structural steel and other pieces of equipment. These dimensions are important if equipment location drawings have not yet been completed. Most often, however, the drafter is given location drawings as a reference showing equipment foundations, anchor bolts, and location dimensions. "Mill Coordinates" are often shown at key locations to provide an overall reference to the "Mill Datum." See Fig. 6-6.

Piping should be dimensioned at each direction change. Dimensions should follow the pipe from its beginning to its end. Dimensions have been added to the drawing in Fig. 6-6. Note the type of dimensioning used. Distances are shown in feet and inches, and the dimension is written above the line on horizontal dimensions and to the left of the line on vertical dimensions.

One other set of features should be dimensioned. These are the structural steel columns that comprise the skeletons of buildings or the vertical members of pipe racks. Note in Fig. 6-6 that dimensions between these steel columns have been added, and the columns have been labeled. These can become important reference points when locating equipment or piping, and when communicating with others about the drawing.

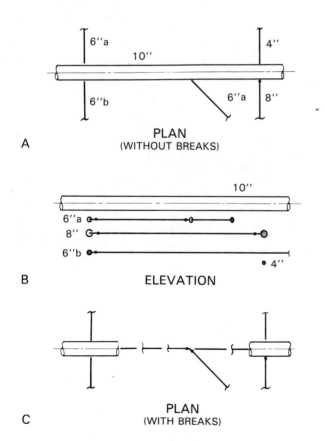

Fig. 6-3. Handling hidden features: A — Piping plan without breaks. B — Elevation of example A. C — Piping plan with breaks.

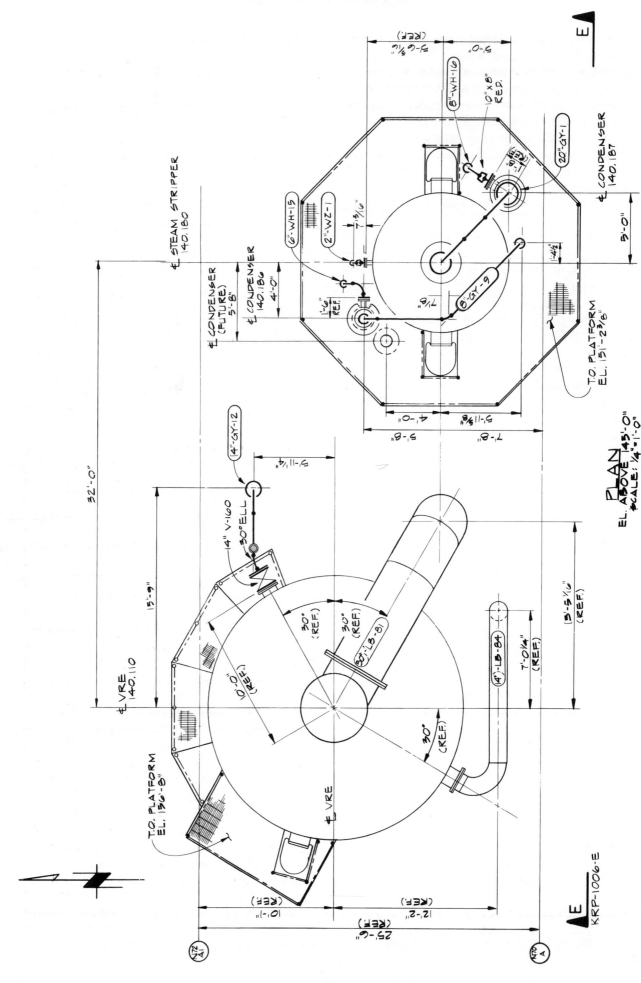

Fig. 6-6. Dimensions and notes are added to plan shown in Fig. 6-2.

74

These structural columns are often referred to as "bay lines" and "column lines," and they are labeled with numbers and letters. Bay lines span the width of a building and column lines run the length. The space between bay lines is referred to as a "bay," which makes sense.

VALVES AND INSTRUMENT PLACEMENT

The flow diagram or P & I diagram becomes the

SCIP NO. A034– 256-1

BASIC DATA	*	MANUFACTURER	FIG. NO.	AVAIL. SIZES	CONSTRUCTION			MATERIALS			
					BONNET	DISC	SEAT	BODY	DISC.	SEAT	STEM
VALVE NO.		CENTERLINE	LT-HO	2-4	INTEG.	SOLID	MOLDED	MEEHA-NITE	NI. PL. IRON	EPT	304 SS
V-520		CENTERLINE	LT-CLG	6-30	INTEG.	SOLID	MOLDED	MEEHA-NITE	NI. PL. IRON	EPT	304 SS
TYPE		CRANE	23N-GRZ T92	2-6	INTEG.	SOLID	MOLDED	NODULAR IRON	NI.RES. IRON	EPT	304 SS
B'FLY		CRANE	23N-GRZ S93	2-10	INTEG.	SOLID	MOLDED	NODULAR IRON	NI.RES. IRON	EPT	304 SS
CONNECT.		DEZURIK	632LDRS 666KGLI	2-4	INTEG.	SOLID	RET. RING	SEMI STEEL	SEMI STEEL	EPT	316 SS
THRD. LUG		DEZURIK	632LDRS 666KEGL	6-20	INTEG.	SOLID	RET. RING	SEMI STEEL	SEMI STEEL	EPT	316 SS
PRESS. RATING		KEYSTONE	122-080 -401	2-4 ⚠	INTEG.	SOLID	MOLDED	NODULAR IRON	NODULAR IRON	EPDM	316 SS
150 W		KEYSTONE	122-080 -417	6-20	INTEG.	SOLID	MOLDED	NODULAR IRON	NODULAR IRON	EPDM ⚠	316 SS
VALVE NO.		CENTERLINE	LT-HO	2-4	INTEG.	SOLID	MOLDED	MEEHA-NITE	316 SS	EPT	316 SS
V-521		CENTERLINE	LT-CLG	6-30	INTEG.	SOLID	MOLDED	MEEHA-NITE	316 SS	EPT	316 SS
TYPE		CRANE	23N-SSZ T92	2-6	INTEG.	SOLID	MOLDED	NODULAR IRON	316 SS	EPT	316 SS
B'FLY		CRANE	23N-SSZ S93	2-10	INTEG.	SOLID	MOLDED	NODULAR IRON	316 SS	EPT	316 SS
CONNECT.		DEZURIK	632LDRS 663KGL1	2-4	INTEG.	SOLID	RET. RING	SEMI STEEL	316 SS	EPT	315 SS
THRD. LUG		DEZURIK	632LDRS 663KEGL	6-20	INTEG.	SOLID	RET. RING	SEMI STEEL	316 SS	EPT	316 SS
PRESS. RATING		KEYSTONE	122-804 -401	2-4	INTEG.	SOLID	MOLDED	NODULAR IRON	316 SS	EPDM	316 SS
150 W		KEYSTONE	122-804 -417	6-20	INTEG.	SOLID	MOLDED	NODULAR IRON	316 SS	EPDM	316 SS
VALVE NO.		CENTERLINE	AA-HO	2-4	INTEG.	SOLID	MOLDED	MEEHA-NITE	NI.PL. IRON	EPT	304 SS
V-522		CENTERLINE	AA-CLG	6-30	INTEG.	SOLID	MOLDED	MEEHA-NITE	NI.PL. IRON	EPT	304 SS
TYPE		CRANE	21F-GRZ T92	2-6	INTEG.	SOLID	MOLDED	NODULAR IRON	NI.RES. IRON	EPT	304 SS
B'FLY		CRANE	21F-GRZ S93	2-10	INTEG.	SOLID	MOLDED	NODULAR IRON	NI.RES. IRON	EPT	304 SS
CONNECT.		DEZURIK	632WDRS 666KGLI	2-24	INTEG.	SOLID	BONDED/ REMOV.	SEMI STEEL	SEMI STEEL	EPT	316 SS
WAFER		DEZURIK	632WRS 666KEGL	6-20	INTEG.	SOLID	BONDED/ REMOV.	SEMI STEEL	SEMI STEEL	EPT	316 SS
PRESS. RATING		KEYSTONE	100-	2-4	INTEG.	SOLID	MOLDED	NODULAR IRON	NODULAR IRON	EPDM	304 SS
150 W		KEYSTONE	100-	6-20	INTEG.	SOLID	MOLDED	NODULAR IRON	NODULAR IRON	EPDM	304 SS

* THESE VALVES WILL BE USED FOR THIS PROJECT. ALTERNATE MUST HAVE APPROVAL OF THE PROJECT ENGINEER.

Fig. 6-7. Chart lists valve specifications from project standards. (Sandwell International, Inc.)

principal reference for finding the number and placement of valves and instruments. You also need to use the project specifications to determine the type of valves used on specific pipes, and the type of connections needed for different instruments. Fig. 6-7 is an example of valve specifications. Valves should be drawn to scale and located in the best possible position for easy access. Instruments are shown as a circle with the code and loop number inside.

Valves in a straight run of pipe should be located with a dimension. This dimension should be to the face of the mating flange as shown in example A in Fig. 6-8. Valves that are attached to fittings do not normally have to be dimensioned because it is a ''fitting-to-fitting'' assembly. See example B in Fig. 6-8.

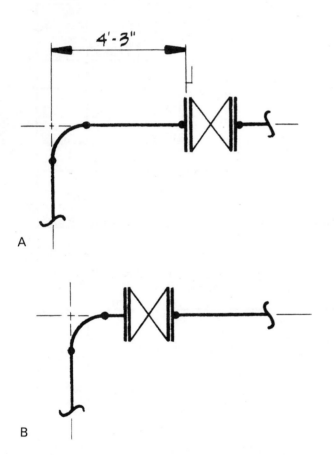

Fig. 6-8. Locating valves: A — Valve in pipe run, dimension required. B — Fitting-to-fitting assembly, no dimension required.

Seldom do instruments have to be located with a dimension. A common exception is the flow meter or ORIFICE FLANGE, Fig. 6-9. This unit is basically two flanges with a plate inserted between them. The plate has a small hole in the center, and its size

is determined by the fluid within the pipe. Each flange has a pressure sensing device inserted into a tapped hole. These devices measure the pressure difference on either side of the orifice plate which can then be converted to the flow rate of the pipe. A minimum amount of turbulence within the pipe is required for this measurement. Therefore, a certain amount of straight pipe is required before the orifice plate. This dimension is noted in the specifications as ''X number of pipe diameters.'' It appears on the piping plan as shown in Fig. 6-10.

Fig. 6-9. Orifice flange has tapped holes in flanges on either side of orifice plate for installation of pressure sensing devices.

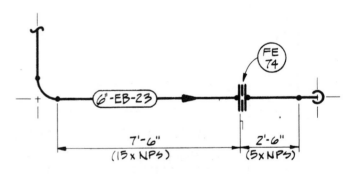

Fig. 6-10. Portion of piping plan gives proper location and dimensioning of orifice plate in straight pipe run.

NOTES AND ABBREVIATIONS

After dimensions, NOTES are the most revealing aspect of the piping plan. Notes and callouts explain and describe things. ABBREVIATIONS are often a big part of the notes. General notes, of course, are shown to one side of the drawing. Local notes identify individual items on the drawing.

Notes should be added to the drawing after the dimensions have been placed. Remember, dimensions are important and should be given preference.

Notes and callouts should be located as close as possible to where they apply. Avoid long leader lines from the note. Fig. 6-11 shows proper location of local notes.

Appendix A in the back of the book contains common abbreviations used in the process piping industry. Use this reference regularly and become familiar with these standard forms. They can save space and time.

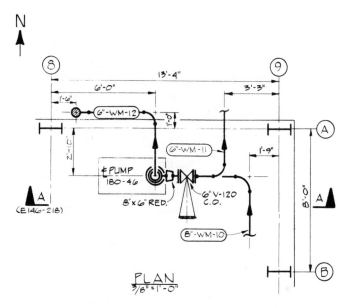

Fig. 6-11. Piping plan shows dimensions, notes, and specifications.

PIPE SPECIFICATIONS AND SYMBOLS

Pipes are identified on the piping plans in the same manner as on the flow diagram. The PIPE SPECIFICATION SYMBOLS should be placed directly in the pipe. If no space is available, place the symbol near the pipe and point to it with a leader. The pipe spec symbols should be one of the last things to be placed on the drawing. While you're at it, don't forget to insert some flow arrows. Fig. 6-11 shows the placement of this information.

SECTION NOTATIONS

You must determine where SECTIONS (elevations) are needed in order to show additional details of the piping system. Sections are indicated on the piping plan with cutting plane lines. See Fig. 6-11. Cutting plane lines have large arrows which point in the direction of view. Sections are identified by a letter. If the section is placed on another drawing, then the letter is accompanied by the number

of that drawing. See Fig. 6-11.

Since we're on the subject, let's take a look at the characteristics of piping elevations.

PIPING ELEVATIONS

ELEVATIONS are also referred to as ''sections.'' Either term is acceptable. These views add another important dimension to our piping drawings. With sections, we can determine vertical features, dimensions, and relationships. Although the drawing techniques and use of symbols is the same as in plans, dimensions for heights are handled differently in sections.

SECTION IDENTIFICATION

The section is always labeled on the plan view, and the same label appears beneath the section where it is drawn. You have seen how the cutting plane line is placed and labeled on the plan view. Now note Fig. 6-12, which shows a section from Fig. 6-11. The subtitle carries the same label and also the number of the drawing on which it was cut. This number becomes especially important when the section is placed on a different drawing.

BEGINNING THE LAYOUT

Sections may be drawn at the same scale as the plan or larger, depending on the required amount of detail to be shown. Most sections are the same scale as the plan. If you are not confident in choosing the locations of sections, your supervisor will do it for you. But in any situation, a logical view to

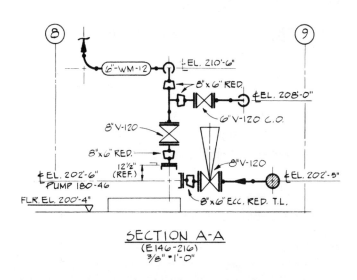

Fig. 6-12. Piping Section A-A taken from Fig. 6-11 includes notes, elevations, and specifications.

choose is the one on the plan that shows the best view of the equipment, such as A-A in Fig. 6-12. After that, the number and locations of sections depends on the amount of detail left to show.

EQUIPMENT LAYOUT

First, determine the size of the section and define these limits on your drawing. This enables you to balance the section on your sheet and give you an idea of how much room you have for other sections. Then, begin your layout in the same manner that you did the plan. Draw the centerlines of equipment lightly at first.

If your section is to show the ground, then you will have to know the heights of the equipment from the ground or floor. Vendor drawings supply this data. Equipment outlines can then be drawn in lightly. Pump outlines may be drawn or only a centerline can be shown. Check your standards.

Centerlines are the most important feature. Pump suction and discharge flanges are shown, as are the reference dimensions to those flanges. Fig. 6-12 shows a typical elevation view of a centrifugal pump. You may remember this from Chapter 4. Note that an elevation is given for the pump centerline instead of a dimension from the floor. This is a common aspect of piping sections. We will see more of this later.

After you have drawn the outlines of all the equipment, begin locating the nozzles. Consult tank and vessel drawings and vendor drawings to find this information. Also check structural drawings showing foundations, pads, grout, etc. This is important data that eventually will give you exact elevations for all the nozzles on the equipment.

PIPING LAYOUT

Now, piping can be drawn, beginning with the highest nozzles. Draw light centerlines at first because you may have to erase a pipe and move it two or three times. This also is a good argument for doing sketches beforehand.

You should note at this point that it is impossible for this text to teach you *all* the finer points of routing pipe. You will not be expected to do this if you are hired on with no previous experience. Laying out piping runs using only flow diagrams and equipment drawings is an art that is developed after many painful hours of erasing and several forays to the construction site to view the actual installation.

An important point to remember is that different line specifications will call for different materials such as pipe, flanges, valves, fittings, etc. There-

fore, always check the project specifications before drawing or dimensioning any new pipes.

STRUCTURAL FEATURES

Elevations often reveal features that are not part of the piping system, but they are vital to its existence. These may be foundations, pads, structural steel columns, ladders, and platforms to name a few. Fig. 6-13 is Section E-E in Fig. 6-6, and it illustrates a few of these features. The nature of the equipment and the location will determine the structural features that are included in your elevation views. These features are referred to as "background information." They are often drawn with a thinner weight line than the pipe.

Pipe racks are steel structures that carry piping and conduit throughout the plant. Think of them as "pipe highways." Fig. 6-14 is an elevation view of a typical pipe rack.

Color in concrete walls, pads, and foundations that have been cut through or marked with the symbol for concrete. Footings and foundations below grade level may be shown with dashed lines. These techniques are shown in Fig. 6-15.

DIMENSIONING

Few, if any, linear dimensions appear on piping elevations. Instead, heights of pipe are noted as elevations. Fig. 6-16 gives some examples. The elevation is not necessarily just the height off the floor or ground. Most industrial sites maintain an established "datum" elevation that is preserved by a monument or marker of some sort. The elevation above sea level of this point is known and used throughout the entire site as a reference. All elevations relate to this point.

If the elevation of a pipe is 14 ft.-10 in. above the datum and the datum is 564 ft.-3 in., what is the elevation of the pipe? You guessed it: 579 ft.-1 in. Some plants and mills will use a false elevation of 100 ft. instead of the actual elevation. This gives an even number from which to measure, and it also insures that all underground elevations within the site are positive figures.

You should be aware of the elevations needed on a piping section. Some elevations must be given to the centerline, while others should be given to the top or bottom. Examples of both are shown in Fig. 6-14. Platforms, floors, steel beams, concrete pads, or foundations are often noted with an elevation on the top of the feature. Pipe in a pipe rack will often be located with an elevation that says "B.O.P." (bottom of pipe). See Fig. 6-14. The bottom of the pipe rests on a piece of steel, so the elevation of the bottom and not the centerline is important.

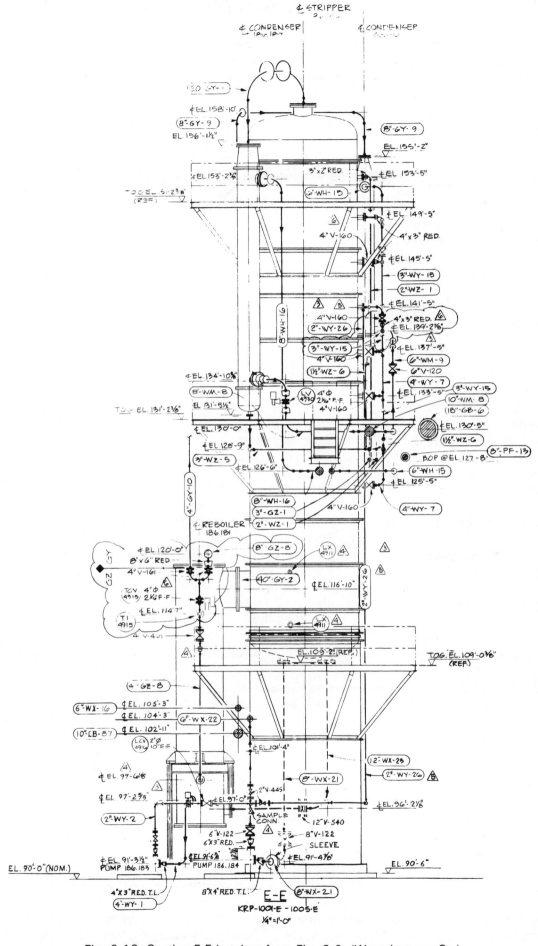

Fig. 6-13. Section E-E is taken from Fig. 6-6. (Weyerhaeuser Co.)

79

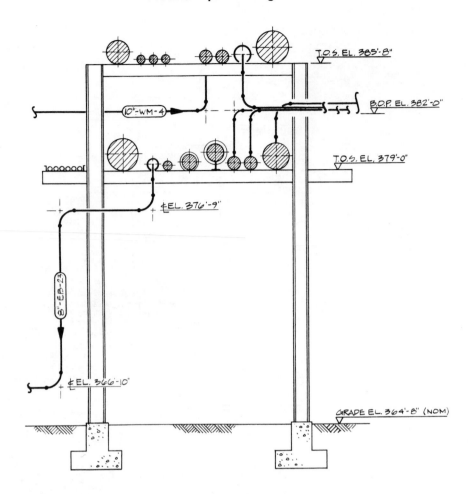

Fig. 6-14. Elevation view of a pipe rack illustrates structural features.

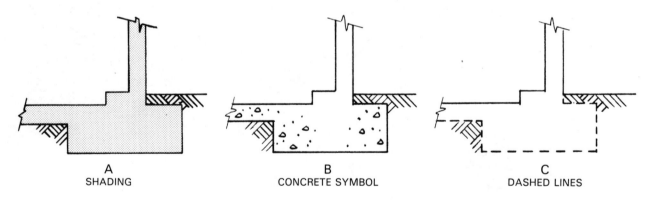

A
SHADING

B
CONCRETE SYMBOL

C
DASHED LINES

Fig. 6-15. Concrete foundations below grade are shown in section.

DRAWING TIPS

In your effort to create a neat and easily understood drawing, there are certain things you need to keep in mind. These include: adhering to company standards; maintaining good line contrast; checking and cross-checking your work; and spelling all words correctly.

STANDARDS

First of all, you should be familiar with your school or company standards and use that information to construct your drawings. When you're not sure of a symbol size or equipment shape, consult the standards. The company standards set a consistency of style for *all* company process pipe drawings, regardless who did the actual drafting.

Often a client demands that certain standards be adhered to that deviate from a company's standards. These are noted and compiled into a set of "project specifications" that are used for the specific project in question. These project specs supercede a company's standards and should be followed closely.

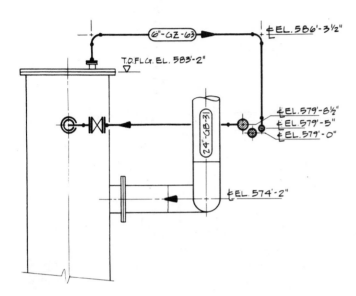

Fig. 6-16. Heights are indicated as "elevations."

LINE CONTRAST

Keep in mind the purpose of your drawings. Remember that the most important aspect of piping drawing — and often the most overlooked — is the pipe. For this reason, you need good line contrast to make the pipe stand out visually on your drawings. Your eyes should be drawn to the piping, especially single line piping.

Also, if the pipe is welded, the weld dots should plainly show. Don't skimp on the weld dots. Someone eventually must count them for estimating and bidding purposes.

CHECKING

Don't leave the checking to the checker. Have mercy. One day you may be a checker. Check your work as you go. Periodically review what you have done. Check your work for drawing errors or inaccurate measurements. Cross-check your line specifications on the piping drawings with the flow diagrams. Make sure they correspond. Check for any intereferences. There always will be in-

terferences, and if you don't find them, the checker will. If the checker doesn't find them, the pipefitter will; and that's when the cost begins to exceed the estimate.

SPELLING

One last thing: keep a dictionary with your reference materials. If you are uncertain how a word is spelled, look it up in the dictionary. Remember: misspelled words on blueprints look "tacky;" blueprints represent your company; spell those words correctly!

Steam stripper column at left is a rear view of one shown in Fig. 6-13. (Weyerhaeuser Co.)

REVIEW QUESTIONS

1. Briefly describe the steps involved in the initial layout of equipment and pipe on a piping plan. _____
_____
_____
_____
_____
_____

2. How does a drafter check for clearances in a congested area? _____

_____

_____

3. What features are equipment dimensioned to?

   a. _____

   b. _____

   c. _____

4. What are the structural steel columns of a building called? _____

   a. _____

   b. _____

5. What type of instrument must be dimensioned within the pipe run? Why? _____

_____

_____

_____

6. How does the drafter determine the location and number of valves on the piping plan?

_____

7. How is the location of a section determined?

_____

_____

_____

8. Who determines the location of a section?

_____

9. What type of information must the drafter refer to in order to properly locate nozzles on the elevation views?

   a. _____

   b. _____

10. How does the presentation of background information differ from the actual piping?

_____

_____

11. How are vertical dimensions handled on a piping section? _____

_____

_____

_____

12. Describe the difference between "project specifications" and "company standards."

_____

_____

_____

_____

PROBLEMS

PROB. 6-1. Redraw the engineering sketches in Figs. Prob. 6-1A and Prob. 6-1B as a single line plan and elevation. Choose your scale and use B size vellum.

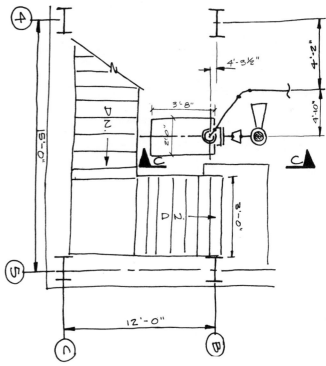

Fig. Prob. 6-1A

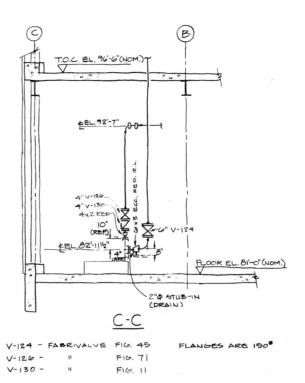

C-C

V-124 — FABRIVALVE FIG. 45   FLANGES ARE 150#

V-126 —   "   FIG. 71

V-130 —   "   FIG. 11

Fig. Prob. 6-1B

PROB. 6-2. Figs. Prob. 6-2A and Prob. 6-2B are elevation views of pipe and fitting assemblies. Complete the four orthographic views of each in the spaces provided.

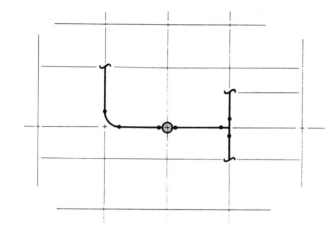

Fig. Prob. 6-2A

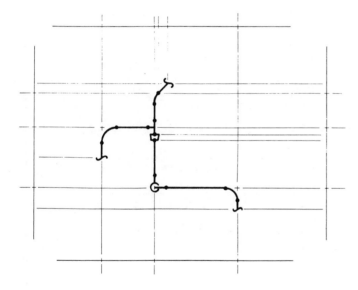

Fig. Prob. 6-2B

PROB. 6-3. Redraw Fig. 6-11 at 3/8″ = 1′ - 0″ scale. Shift the pump discharge 10 1/2″ toward column line "B." Show the 6″ line with the C.O. valve going to the left (instead of right as shown) for 4′, then turning north. On the same sheet, draw the section in Fig. 6-12 to reflect the above changes.

PROB. 6-4. Fill in the missing elevations in Fig. Prob. 6-4. Use the appendix to find necessary valve dimensions. Flanges are 300# and gaskets are 1/8″ thick. Be sure to note the eccentric reducer.

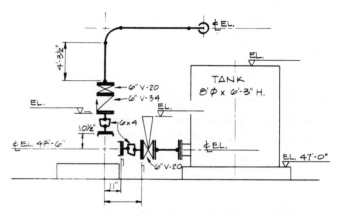

V-20 – JENKINS FIG. 1325
V-34 – CRANE NO. 383

Fig. Prob. 6-4

Chapter 7

NOTES, ABBREVIATIONS, AND REVISIONS

NOTES are an essential part of piping drawings. A world of information is contained within them, so it is important that they are written correctly.

Notes are often "peppered" with ABBREVIATIONS which, if used properly, can save drafting time and space on the drawing.

REVISIONS (changes, deletions, corrections) on the other hand, are looked upon with scorn by many drafters because it means erasing portions of their drawings. However, revisions are a vital part of the design process, though sometimes carried to the extreme by over-zealousness and carelessness.

In this chapter, we will look at notes, abbreviations, the purpose of revisions, and the manner in which they are handled on drawings. We will see why notes are necessary; who decides what goes in the general notes; how local notes differ from general notes; and why revisions occur.

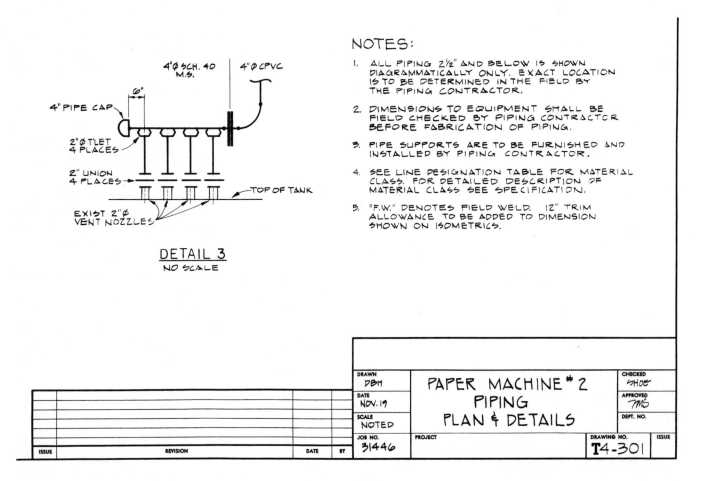

Fig. 7-1. This piping drawing presents a good example of proper layout for general notes.

NOTES

NOTES on pipe drawings consist of general notes, local notes, valve labels, and miscellaneous labels such as pipe specifications and flow arrows.

GENERAL NOTES

Any drafter knows that GENERAL NOTES refer to the entire drawing and that they "congregate" around the edges of drawings. Most often they are found in the area above the title block or along the bottom of the drawing. Seldom does the junior drafter have to decide what goes in the general notes. The engineer, designer, or lead drafter determines the information needed here. If located above the title block, the heading "NOTES" should be placed high enough above it to leave room for future notes. Fig. 7-1 is an example of a good layout for general notes.

LOCAL NOTES

LOCAL NOTES are more specific than general notes, and they are found "sitting" very near the place where they apply. A local note applies only to the part or area pointed out by its leader line. When placing the note on the drawing, keep it as close as possible to the part it refers to. Fig. 7-2 shows acceptable placement of local notes.

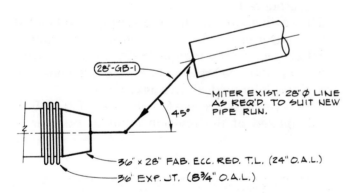

Fig. 7-2. Double line drawing shows care in selection of locations for local notes.

Notes are nice, but they must be limited to only necessary information. Most companies label only odd fittings. They leave common ones such as 90° elbows, straight tees, weld neck flanges, and slip-on flanges to fend for themselves. For instance, all reducers must be labeled, as must reducing tees. A general rule to follow is: "If there be doubt, call it out."

Valves are especially important items to label. Many different kinds of valves may be used in one piping system. If they are not labeled, confusion could result. Most companies establish specifications for each valve type and give that valve its own number. This is the number that is to appear on the piping drawings. Note in Fig. 7-3 that the valves are labeled with different numbers, and pipe diameter is the first part of each label.

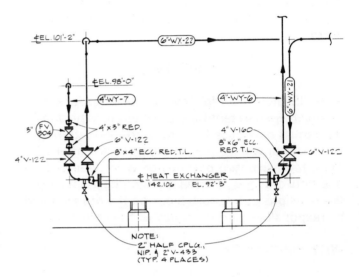

Fig. 7-3. Single line pipe drawing contains many different valves, each properly labeled for identification.

MISCELLANEOUS LABELS

PIPE SPECIFICATIONS and FLOW ARROWS are two items often omitted from drawings through carelessness and haste. Pipe specifications are vital to the interpretation of the piping drawings. Try to place them in a straight run of pipe. If that fails, find an empty space near the pipe and point to it with a leader, Figs. 7-2 and 7-3. Flow arrows add to the clarity of the drawing. Don't forget them.

Notes and labels often appear unintelligible to the untrained, either because of the wording, spelling, or the abbreviations used. Therefore, when writing notes: be brief, write clearly, and above all spell correctly. Most veteran drafters keep a good dictionary on their reference shelf. You would do well to follow this example.

ABBREVIATIONS

ABBREVIATIONS are little shortcuts that can be a great help — or they can cause untold confusion. Appendix A contains an extensive list of abbreviations used in the industry. Each company has a few extra of their own, but that is to be expected. Abbreviations save space on the drawing. Use them wherever possible. Some examples of notes with abbreviations are shown in Figs. 7-2 and 7-3.

Notes and abbreviations sometimes get out of hand. Consider, for example, the lengthy, abbreviated note found on an old blueprint years ago. It read: "Angle brace, C.T.S., B.T.F., P.T.M., S.T.F. & I.A.L." Some research was required to discover the meaning of this message. It was finally deciphered as: "Angle brace, cut to suit, beat to fit, paint to match, ship to field, and install at leisure."

REVISIONS

REVISIONS occur for any number of reasons; few of which are pleasant for the drafter. It is the drafter who must erase the fine line work and lettering it took days or weeks to produce. It is the drafter who must redraw entire portions of what was once a beautiful drawing. It is the drafter who must record the revisions in a special block on the drawing and be responsible for distribution of the revised copy.

WHY REVISIONS?

"Change" is the one certain thing in this world. We can expect that things will change. And they do. Revisions are often the result of a change in the design of a system or part of a system. The change may come about because of a product improvement, client request, design innovation, gross miscalculation, or blunder in drawing. When one of these things happens, it is often up to the drafter to make the necessary alterations to the drawing.

Revisions generally are a vital part of the design process, and it is in your best interest to become aware of that fact as soon as possible. It is difficult to change something that is not yet on paper and can't be seen. But once a system becomes visible to all in a drawing, it is subject to criticism and changes.

REVISION IDENTIFICATION

A preliminary drawing (one not yet approved by the chief engineer) can be changed and altered without recording the changes. But once it has been approved for release to a client, all revisions must be noted on the drawing and logged in a special REVISIONS BLOCK.

The area that is revised is often circled with a "cloud." See Fig. 7-4. This cloud usually is drawn on the back of the drawing to facilitate easy

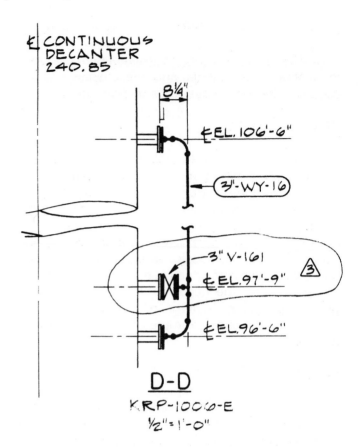

Fig. 7-4. Revised information is encircled by a revision cloud and labeled by a number inside a triangle.

removal. Only the current revision should have a cloud around it.

The revised area on the drawing is also labeled with a letter or number placed inside a geometric symbol, such as the triangle in Fig. 7-4. This symbol remains on the drawing for future reference, but the cloud is erased on the next revision.

The revision block itself is shown in Fig. 7-5. It is composed of the revision letter or number, a

REV	BY DATE	REVISION	APP'D.
4	SHOE 13 Nov. 75	REVISED 4"-GZ-8, ADDED ELEV. & VALVES, ADDED VALVE CALLOUTS.	HACK
3	HACK 28 NOV. 75	REVISED 2"-WY-2, ADDED 2"-WY-24 ON SECTIONS C-C AND E-E.	PLR
2	JCH 8 OCT 75	ADDED TOP WORKS TO TV-4927, TI-4904, FX & FV-4905, SPOOL PIECE & 4"-V-160	HACK
1	JCH 21 SEP 75	RELEASED SECT. C-C	HACK

Fig. 7-5. Revision block identifies and describes revision; also gives date made, who made revision, and who approved it.

description of the revision, the name or initials of the person making the revision, the date made, and the initials of the person who approved the revision. Companies may vary slightly on the information required in the revision block.

The final aspect of the revision is found in the title block, often in the lower right corner. This little block, Fig. 7-6, contains the current revision number, which is handy when searching through files of old blueprints to find a specific revision.

One last warning: Always send the client a copy of the latest revision. It won't do anyone any good if you make the revision and file it away. They may have dug the trench in the wrong area and ruptured a natural gas line. And *you* may be standing in the unemployment line.

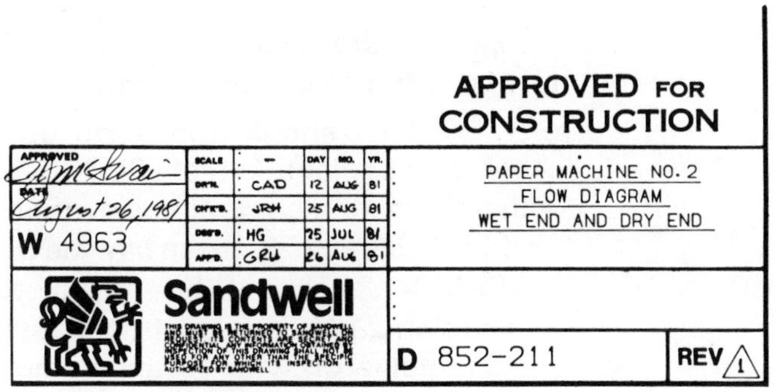

Fig. 7-6. Title block contains current revision number in extreme lower right corner. (Sandwell International, Inc.)

REVIEW QUESTIONS

1. What is the difference between general and local notes? _____
_____
_____
_____

2. Name some fittings that aren't normally called out with a note. _____
_____
_____

3. How are valves identified on a piping drawing? _____
_____
_____

4. Where is the best place to locate pipe specifications? _____
_____
_____

Identify the following abbreviations:

5. CPLG _____
ECC _____
OAL _____
FOB _____

6. NPT _____
RF _____
NOM _____
TE _____

7. SPEC _____
GSKT _____
FW _____
TOE _____

8. BE _____
TL _____
SR _____
PS _____

9. STM _____
TOG _____
MS _____
CFM _____

10. DIA _____
API _____
ISO _____
SO FLG _____

11. CO _____
NIP _____
BC _____
IE _____

12. F-F _____
WOG _____
FDN _____
NTS _____

13. What are revisions? _____
_____

14. Why do revisions occur? _____
_____
_____
_____

15. What is a preliminary drawing? _____
_____

16. How is a revision made to stand out on a drawing? _____
_____
_____

17. What kind of information is found on the revision block? _____

_____

_____

_____

18. What do you think is the most important responsibility of the drafter concerning revisions? _____

_____

_____

PROBLEMS

PROB. 7-1. Interpret the notes in Figs. Prob. 7-1A through 7-1F. Write your answers in the spaces provided.

PROB. 7-2. The following statements are verbal descriptions of simple notes. Print the notes in the spaces provided as they would appear on a piping drawing. Use abbreviations whenever possible.

a. A 6 x 4 eccentric reducer with the bottom surface flat.

_____

b. A weld neck flange, raised faced, with a pressure rating of 300#.

_____

c. A 12″ slip-on flange with a bolt circle of 17″.

_____

d. A 10″ tee with an outlet size of 6″.

_____

e. A 90 degree elbow, short radius, 8″ in diameter, wall thickness of schedule 40.

_____

f. A 3″ nominal pipe size with a beveled end.

_____

g. An orifice flange rated 300# and 6″ in diameter.

_____

PROB. 7-3. Revise your drawing in Fig. Prob. 6-3 to reflect the following changes:

a. 8″-WM-10 should run north at a centerline elevation of 208′-0″, then drop to a centerline elevation of 202′-5″ at 1′-9″ from bay line 9.

b. 6″-WM-12 should be raised to elevation 214′-8″. Construct a revision block on your drawing and record the changes. Draw a cloud around the changes and place the proper revision symbol by the change.

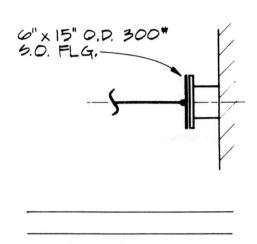

6" x 15" O.D. 300# S.O. FLG.

Fig. Prob. 7-1A

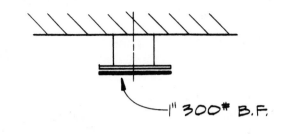

1" 300# B.F.

Fig. Prob. 7-1B

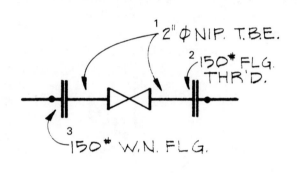

1 2"∅ NIP. T.B.E.

2 150# FLG. THR'D.

3 150# W.N. FLG.

1 _____

2 _____

3 _____

Fig. Prob. 7-1C

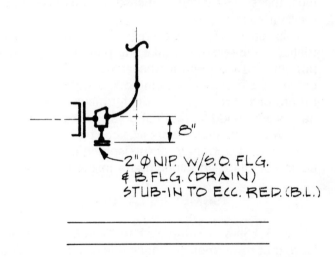

8"

2"∅ NIP. W/S.O. FLG. & B.FLG. (DRAIN) STUB-IN TO ECC. RED. (B.L.)

_____

_____

Fig. Prob. 7-1D

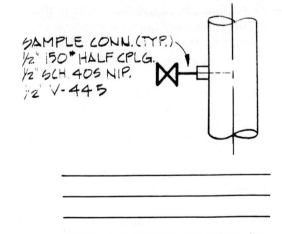

SAMPLE CONN. (TYP.)
1/2" 150# HALF CPLG.
1/2" SCH. 40S NIP.
1/2" V-445

Fig. Prob. 7-1E

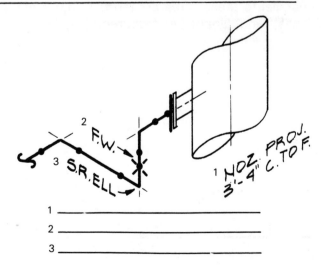

2 F.W.

3 S.R. ELL

1 NOZ. PROJ. 3'-4" C. TO F.

1 _____

2 _____

3 _____

Fig. Prob. 7-1F

Chapter 8

PIPING ISOMETRICS

An ISOMETRIC DRAWING is one in which three sides of an object can be seen in one view. It is a type of pictorial drawing. Unlike perspective drawings, the isometric can be measured and drawn with relative ease.

This ease of measurement and layout, and realistic appearance, make the piping isometric a popular drawing within the industry. Some companies use it in lieu of piping plans and elevations; others use it to supplement the plans. Isometrics can also be used as fabrication and shop drawings from which the pipe assemblies can be constructed. And, most importantly, piping isometrics can be used to calculate angular offsets in the pipe run.

ISOMETRIC LAYOUT

Fig. 8-1 is an example of an ISOMETRIC AXIS. Note that three lines compose this layout: a vertical line and two lines at 30° from horizontal. These three lines, and any other lines that are parallel to them, are called "isometric lines."

Isometric lines *can* be measured. Any lines not parallel to these three are termed "non-isometric lines" and cannot be measured.

Remember the isometric axis? You will use it to lay out *all* of your isometric drawings. Take a look at the simple isometric in Fig. 8-2, and note that all directions of the pipe match the three isometric axis lines. Later, we will see that some lines may deviate from one of the axis lines.

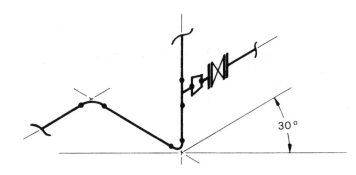

Fig. 8-2. In this simple piping isometric drawing, all piping parallels the three isometric axis lines.

SCALE

Another nice thing about the isometric is that it seldom is drawn to scale. Can you imagine why? But it *is* important to show the pipe lengths in proportion. A 64 ft. section of pipe would appear longer than a 15 ft. piece. The example shown in Fig. 8-3 illustrates this point. Many companies draw isometrics on "B" size paper (11 in. x 17 in.), and space is limited. Because of the lack of scale, however, it is doubly important that the written dimensions are accurate.

DIRECTION AND LOCATION

Location and direction features help to properly orient the isometric drawing. The north arrow gives direction. It should always point to either the top right or top left of the paper, Fig. 8-3. The bay and

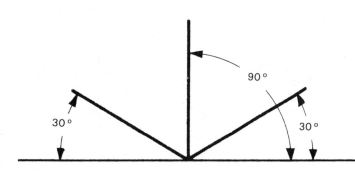

Fig. 8-1. Three lines make up the isometric axes for laying out all isometric drawings.

column line symbols or other structural reference points that provide location are also shown in Fig. 8-3. Dimensions must always be given to these points of reference, but only once in each plane. Mill coordinates may also be shown on the isometric drawing.

ISOMETRIC PLANES

Three planes exist in isometric drawings. Therefore, valves and fittings can be shown in a number of ways. It is up to you to choose the correct orientation. Fig. 8-4 illustrates the three planes and possible positions of fittings and valves.

FITTING SYMBOLS AND ORIENTATION

Fig. 8-5 shows both good and bad methods of orienting fittings. A general rule to use is to draw the fittings so that they are parallel to the last direction change or branch in the pipe. It tends to give continuity between the planes.

Fittings are drawn the same shape as they appear on the plans and elevations except that they are shown at an isometric angle. See Figs. 8-4 and 8-5. Remember that elbows can be drawn a couple of ways, so check your company or school standards before you draw. Example A in Fig. 8-6 shows elbows represented as curved. This is a bit more realistic than example B, which depicts them with square corners. The square corner method is used more often because it is quicker to draw. Note the correct isometric ellipse orientation indicated in example A in Fig. 8-6.

CONNECTED PIPING

Most companies show only one run of pipe per isometric drawing. However, many pipes have branches and/or "tributaries." These generally are shown with a dashed line for a short distance past the main run. See Fig. 8-7. A note is used to indicate the name or specification of the branch pipe.

Existing piping is often shown by using the double line method, as in Fig. 8-7. This technique is

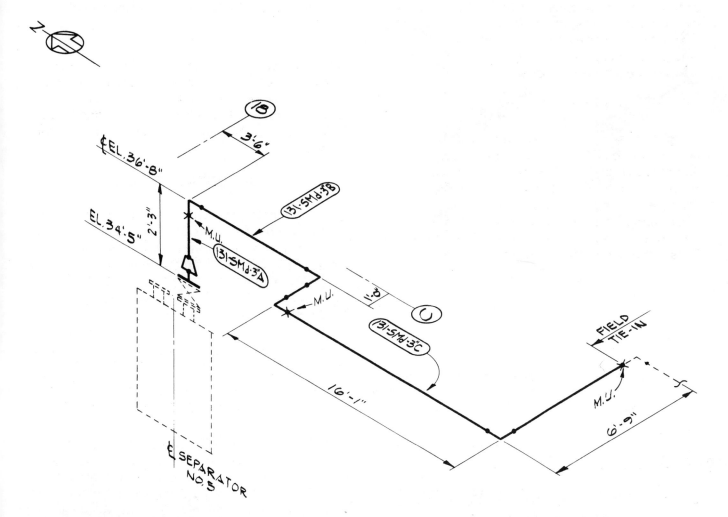

Fig. 8-3. Single line isometric piping drawing illustrates the need for various pipe lengths to be drawn in proportion.

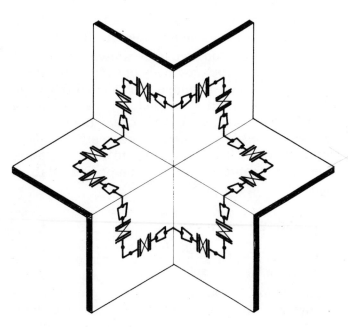

Fig. 8-4. Fitting orientation is shown on the three isometric planes.

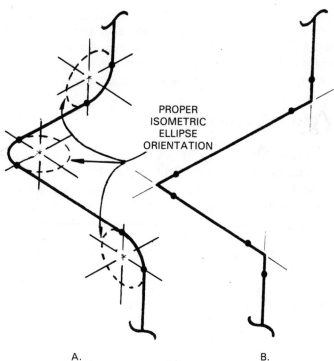

PROPER ISOMETRIC ELLIPSE ORIENTATION

A.   B.

Fig. 8-6. These piping isometrics have curved elbow representation at A and square corner representation at B.

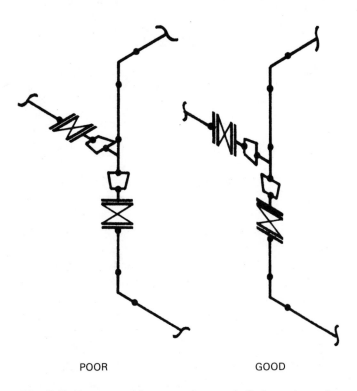

POOR   GOOD

Fig. 8-5. Proper and improper isometric fitting orientation is illustrated in these examples. Note the parallelism of lines and fitting symbols in the good example.

useful in that it distinguishes new from existing piping.

DRAWING ISOMETRIC OFFSETS

An "offset" is just *that.* The pipe is moved from one direction line to another. This is done with a fitting, usually a 45° elbow. It may be necessary for you to use what some refer to as "artistic license," and what others term the "fudge factor." Refer to Fig. 8-8 as you study the following examples.

HORIZONTAL OFFSETS

A horizontal pipe with a "45" running from southeast to northwest, if drawn technically correct, would appear as a vertical line. Since this could create confusion, the offset is drawn 22 1/2° from vertical to give the illusion of the angle. See example A in Fig. 8-8. But, as we see in example B, an offset drawn technically correct in the opposite direction would be acceptable. "Squaring-in" lines shown in example A are helpful in establishing which plane the piping is in.

VERTICAL OFFSETS

VERTICAL OFFSETS can appear particularly confusing if you neglect to follow some of the suggestions given here. Refer to examples C through F in Fig. 8-8. A vertical pipe with an offset to the south and up, if drawn technically correct, would appear as an east-west horizontal run. The angle should be

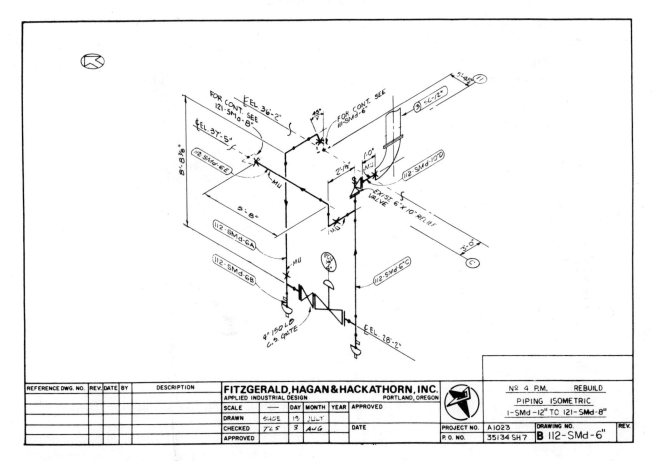

Fig. 8-7. Isometric drawing shows connected piping. New piping is single line; existing piping is double line. (Fitzgerald, Hagan & Hackathorn, Inc.)

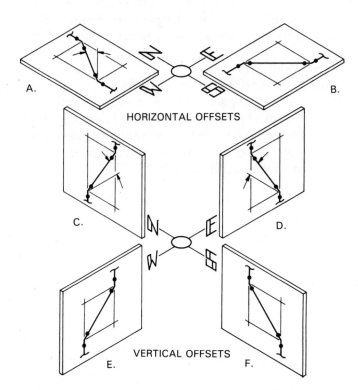

HORIZONTAL OFFSETS

VERTICAL OFFSETS

Fig. 8-8. Proper representation of isometric offsets is illustrated. See explanatory text references.

raised approximately 22 1/2° to give the best appearance. See example C.

Similarly, a vertical pipe having a 45° offset to the west would appear as a north-south horizontal run if drawn technically correct. In this case, rotate the line up 22 1/2°. Example D in Fig. 8-8 depicts this offset.

Examples E and F in Fig. 8-8 show two cases in which the fudge factor does not have to be used. Example E shows a vertical pipe run offset up 45° to the east. When drawn technically correct, it is also isometrically correct. No change is needed.

The same situation is true with a vertical pipe that is offset 45° down to the south. This particular vertical offset is technically correct as drawn in example F in Fig. 8-8. It is also isometrically correct. No artistic alterations are needed.

You should constantly be aware of some of the confusing qualities inherent in isometric piping drawings, and always take measures to insure that these drawings are easily understood. One of these measures is to draw in all squaring lines (centerlines) that represent the pipe run if only 90° ells were used in the run.

CALCULATING ISOMETRIC OFFSETS

When drawing offsets, you can often get by with an educated guess. But when determining pipe lengths and angles of the offset, precise calculations enter the picture. It is important that any beginning pipe drafter develop a working knowledge of right angle trigonometry.

FINDING UNKNOWN SIDES

Let's look at how trigonometry applies to pipe drafting. The pipe in Fig. 8-9 rises at a 45° angle, then "bends" again to go vertically upward. We know the measurements of two sides, a and b, but need to determine the pipe length of side c. We can calculate this by using the following formula:

$$c = \sqrt{a^2 + b^2}$$

By substituting the given measurements into the formula, and converting the fractions to decimals, we can solve for c:

$$c = 5'\text{-}6\ 1/4''^2 + 5\text{-}'6\ 1/4''^2$$
$$c = (5.5208)^2 + (5.5208)^2$$
$$c = 30.4792 + 30.4792$$
$$c = 60.9585$$
$$c = 7'\text{-}9\ 11/16''$$

We know that the two perpendicular sides of a 45° triangle are equal. Normally, the elevation of 443'-0 3/4'' would not appear on a piping draw-

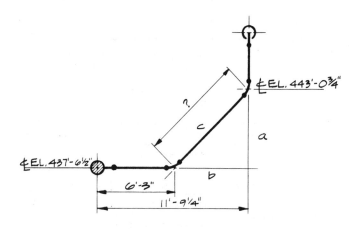

Fig. 8-9. Common 45° offset problem is presented in text reference. Find pipe length of side c.

ing. It is shown here for clarity only.

The formula you just "stepped" through was theorized in the 6th century B.C. by Greek philosopher Pythagoras. He concluded that the square of the hypotenuse is equal to the sum of the squares of the two sides. The hypotenuse is always the side opposite the 90° angle. Fig. 8-10 illustrates the sides of a triangle and gives the three combinations of the "Pythagorean Theorem."

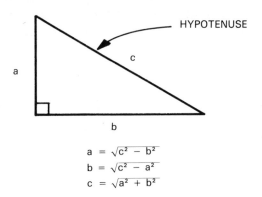

$$a = \sqrt{c^2 - b^2}$$
$$b = \sqrt{c^2 - a^2}$$
$$c = \sqrt{a^2 + b^2}$$

Fig. 8-10. Pythagorean theorem formulas are given for right triangle sides.

FROM SMOLEY'S TO CALCULATORS

In 1901, an educator and civil engineer named Constantine K. Smoley ("C.K." to his devotees) published a thick gilded book called SMOLEY'S TABLES. This book soon became the "bible" for engineers, architects, and students who needed to calculate squares, square roots, logarithms, and trigonometric functions. Well-worn, floppy, dog-eared copies occupied prime spots for years on the desks of engineers and architects worldwide. Smoley had taken the "wet" out of "sweat."

These days that spot on the desk is occupied by powerful pocket calculators and microcomputers. Smoley's volume shaved hours of calculations from engineering tasks, and now the new breed of calculators and computers has shaved hours off of thumbing through Smoley's.

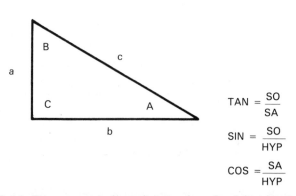

$$TAN = \frac{SO}{SA}$$
$$SIN = \frac{SO}{HYP}$$
$$COS = \frac{SA}{HYP}$$

Fig. 8-11. Trigonometric formulas are given for right triangle angles.

However, lest our squares and roots be forgotten, you are urged to become familiar with SMOLEY'S TABLES, especially the sections on logarithms and squares, logarithms of trigonometric functions, and natural functions. These are/were the sections used most frequently by pipe drafters. You never know when your calculator battery is going to expire.

FINDING UNKNOWN ANGLES

Three basic "trig" function formulas are used frequently in piping. See Fig. 8-11. When angle A is used, a is the side opposite (SO) and b is the side adjacent (SA). When angle B is used, a is the side adjacent and b is the side opposite.

The angle "A" is required in Fig. 8-12. Follow the steps on the drafter's worksheet to determine the angle. Then, using the correct Pythagorean Theorem formula given in Fig. 8-10, solve for the length of side "c."

A more complete list of formulas is shown in Fig. 8-13. Again, familiarize yourself with these formulas in solving for angles and lengths in piping offsets.

Solving for angles may be done by using logarithms or "natural functions." Feet and inches must be converted to decimals, and the natural functions table of Smoley's can be used to convert your answers. The table in Fig. 8-14 is provided for this purpose. The solution to Fig. 8-12 using natural functions is shown in Fig. 8-15.

SOLVING COMPOUND ANGLES

Piping must often be snaked through a hissing, vibrating chaos of equipment, steel, conduit, and pipe. When this occurs, the pipe may be "rolled" along with the offset. This is termed a "rolling offset" in piping parlance. It forms a "compound angle." The example in Fig. 8-16 is typical of a

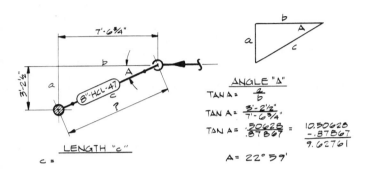

Reader's Calculations

Fig. 8-12. Trigonometric calculations are shown on pipe drafter's worksheet. Follow steps under ANGLE "A" and solve for pipe length of side "c."

FORMULAS FOR RIGHT ANGLED TRIANGLES

$$a = \sqrt{c^2 - b^2}$$
$$b = \sqrt{c^2 - a^2}$$
$$c = \sqrt{a^2 + b^2}$$

KNOWN	REQUIRED					
	A	B	a	b	c	Area
a, b	$\text{Tan A} = \dfrac{a}{b}$	$\text{Tan B} = \dfrac{b}{a}$			$\sqrt{a^2 + b^2}$	$\dfrac{ab}{2}$
a, c	$\text{Sin A} = \dfrac{a}{c}$	$\text{Cos B} = \dfrac{a}{c}$		$\sqrt{c^2 - a^2}$		$\dfrac{a\sqrt{c^2 - a^2}}{2}$
A, a		$90° - A$		a Cot A	$\dfrac{a}{\text{Sin A}}$	$\dfrac{a^2 \text{ Cot A}}{2}$
A, b		$90° - A$	b Tan A		$\dfrac{b}{\text{Cos A}}$	$\dfrac{b^2 \text{ Tan A}}{2}$
A, c		$90° - A$	c Sin A	C Cos		$\dfrac{C^2 \text{ Sin 2A}}{4}$

Fig. 8-13. Formulas are listed for right angled triangles.
Study the workings of these formulas.

	Decimals of a Foot												Decimals of an inch
	0"	1"	2"	3"	4"	5"	6"	7"	8"	9"	10"	11"	
	.000	.0833	.1667	.2500	.3333	.4167	.5000	.5833	.6667	.7500	.8333	.9167	—	
1/16"	.0052	.0885	.1719	.2552	.3385	.4219	.5052	.5885	.6719	.7552	.8385	.9219	1/16"	.0625
1/8"	.0104	.0937	.1771	.2604	.3437	.4271	.5104	.5937	.6771	.7604	.8437	.9271	1/8"	.1250
3/16"	.0156	.0990	.1823	.2656	.3490	.4323	.5156	.5990	.6823	.7656	.8490	.9323	3/16"	.1875
1/4"	.0209	.1042	.1875	.2708	.3542	.4375	.5208	.6042	.6875	.7708	.8542	.9375	1/4"	.2500
5/16"	.0260	.1094	.1927	.2760	.3594	.4427	.5260	.6094	.6927	.7760	.8594	.9427	5/16"	.3125
3/8"	.0312	.1146	.1979	.2812	.3646	.4479	.5312	.6146	.6979	.7812	.8646	.9479	3/8"	.3750
7/16"	.0365	.1198	.2031	.2865	.3698	.4531	.5365	.6198	.7031	.7865	.8698	.9531	7/16"	.4375
1/2"	.0417	.1250	.2083	.2917	.3750	.4583	.5417	.6250	.7083	.7917	.8750	.9583	1/2"	.5000
9/16"	.0469	.1302	.2135	.2969	.3802	.4635	.5469	6.302	.7135	.7969	.8802	.9635	9/16"	.5625
5/8"	.0521	.1354	.2188	.3021	.3854	.4688	.5521	6.354	.7188	.8021	.8854	.9688	5/8"	.6250
11/16"	.0573	.1406	.2240	.3073	.3906	.4740	.5573	.6406	.7240	.8073	.8906	.9740	11/16"	.6875
3/4"	.0625	.1458	.2292	.3125	.3958	.4792	.5625	.6458	.7292	.8125	.8958	.9792	3/4"	.7500
13/16"	.0677	.1510	.2344	.3177	.4010	.4844	.5677	.6510	.7344	.8177	.9010	.9844	13/16"	.8125
7/8"	.0729	.1562	.2396	.3229	.4062	.4896	.5729	.6562	.7396	.8229	.9062	.9896	7/8"	.8750
15/16"	.0781	.1615	.2448	.3281	.4115	.4948	.5781	.6615	.7448	.8281	.9115	9948	15/16"	.9375

Fig. 8-14. Table converts feet and inches to decimals.

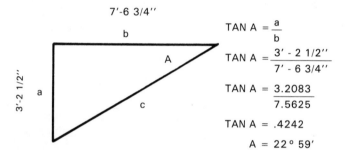

$$TAN\ A = \frac{a}{b}$$

$$TAN\ A = \frac{3'\text{-}2\,1/2''}{7'\text{-}6\,3/4''}$$

$$TAN\ A = \frac{3.2083}{7.5625}$$

$$TAN\ A = .4242$$

$$A = 22° 59'$$

Fig. 8-15. Solution is shown here for problem presented in Fig. 8-12.

drafter's worksheet for a rolling offset.

Four terms are associated with this rolling offset configuration:

RUN: Length of total offset in direction of pipe run.

SET: Depth of offset.

ROLL: Breadth of offset.

TRAVEL: True length of pipe through offset.

The TRAVEL is most often the measurement to be found, and this may involve solving two triangles. Follow the drafter's notes in Fig. 8-16 to find the solution (using natural functions from the table in Fig. 8-14).

Accurate calculations at this point can eliminate unnecessary field fitting, cutting, and welding.

ISOMETRIC DIMENSIONING AND LABELING

Two planes are evident in dimensioning and labeling: horizontal and vertical. Keep in mind the plane of the pipe and dimension line in order to properly orient lettering and dimensions.

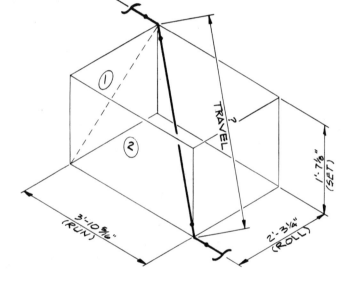

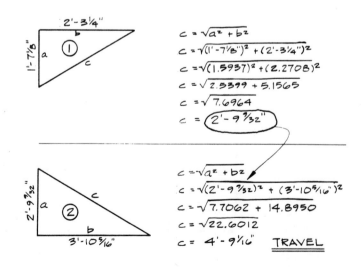

$$c = \sqrt{a^2 + b^2}$$
$$c = \sqrt{(1'\text{-}7\,7/8'')^2 + (2'\text{-}3\,1/4'')^2}$$
$$c = \sqrt{(1.5937)^2 + (2.2708)^2}$$
$$c = \sqrt{2.5399 + 5.1565}$$
$$c = \sqrt{7.6964}$$
$$c = 2'\text{-}9\,9/32''$$

$$c = \sqrt{a^2 + b^2}$$
$$c = \sqrt{(2'\text{-}9\,9/32'')^2 + (3'\text{-}10\,5/16'')^2}$$
$$c = \sqrt{7.7062 + 14.8950}$$
$$c = \sqrt{22.6012}$$
$$c = 4'\text{-}9\,9/16''\quad TRAVEL$$

Fig. 8-16. Compound angle or "rolling offset" solution is worked out on drafter's worksheet.

96

DIMENSIONING PRACTICES

The best way to dimension a pipe is to its centerline at the intersection point. Do not dimension to the pipe unless you must. See example A in Fig. 8-17. Try to keep all dimensions outside the piping view when possible. Vertical dimensions and pipe elevations are also shown. Check your company or school standards.

Dimensions should always be shown between points in the same plane. Measurements given between points in parallel planes are confusing and meaningless. Example B in Fig. 8-17 illustrates this point.

Two final notes about dimensioning:
1. One of the extension lines of the dimension should be a centerline of the run of pipe.
2. When drawing arrowheads, the heel of the arrow should always be parallel to the extension lines. Example A in Fig. 8-17 shows this.

ISOMETRIC LETTERING

Remember the three planes mentioned earlier? They become evident when you begin to label your drawing. The following guidelines will get you started.

If the pipe is vertical, the lettering should be written vertically and at a 30° angle. Fig. 8-18 clearly shows this. If the pipe is in the horizontal plane, the lettering will appear as if it is lying down. It will be oriented on both 30° angles. See Fig. 8-18. Dimensions appear to be lying down if the pipe is horizontal, or standing on end if the pipe is vertical.

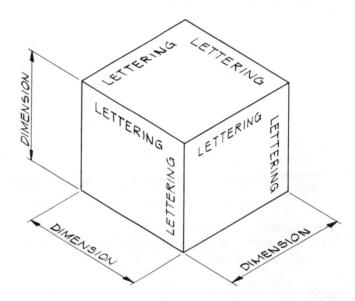

Fig. 8-18. Isometric lettering guidelines are graphically illustrated.

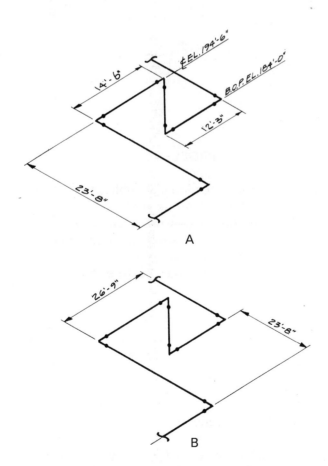

Fig. 8-17. Isometric dimensioning dos and don'ts are illustrated. A — Correct. B — Incorrect.

PIPING ISOMETRIC APPLICATIONS

The purpose of this chapter has been to expose you to common methods used in the construction of piping isometrics. Companies use isometric drawings for various purposes. Some show an entire run of pipe from one piece of equipment to another. Others show an entire piping system in isometric.

Then there are those who show only the amount of piping that will fit in a railroad car or on a flatbed truck. These drawings are often referred to as "isometric spool drawings." The spool is a subassembly of pipe and fittings that is joined to another spool to create an entire run of pipe. The subject of "spools" will be covered in the next chapter.

Turn to page 98 for Review Questions and Problems.

REVIEW QUESTIONS

1. What is meant by ''isometric lines'' and ''non-isometric lines?'' _____
_____
_____
_____

2. Sketch the three isometric axes and label the angle from horizontal of each.

3. Why do you think that piping isometrics are seldom drawn to scale? _____
_____
_____

4. Sketch the two ways that 90° elbows can be drawn isometrically.

5. What is an offset? _____
_____
_____

6. What are squaring-in lines and why are they used? _____
_____

7. Who was C.K. Smoley and what is he known for? _____
_____
_____
_____

8. When do trigonometric formulas have to be used in pipe drafting? _____
_____

9. What is a rolling offset? _____
_____
_____
_____

10. Define the following terms:
RUN: _____
_____
SET: _____
_____
ROLL: _____
_____
TRAVEL: _____
_____

11. Sketch a one inch isometric cube below, and letter the words ''top,'' ''front,'' and ''side'' on the appropriate planes in isometric lettering. Dimension the cube.

PROBLEMS

PROB. 8-1. Draw the pipe assemblies in Fig. Prob. 3-4 in isometric form.

PROB. 8-2. In the spaces provided, draw piping isometrics of each arrangement shown in examples A through D in Fig. Prob. 8-2. These can be freehand or done with a straightedge.

PROB. 8-3. Draw an isometric of the four pipe assemblies in Fig. Prob. 8-2 on C size drawing paper. Show all dimensions, elevations, and callouts. Use standard dimensions for gate valves.

PROB. 8-4. Redraw the piping assemblies in Fig. Prob. 8-2 from two other viewpoints. Your drawings must be isometric.

PROB. 8-5. Solve the problems in examples A through E in Fig. Prob. 8-5 for the unknown value indicated. Write your answers in the spaces provided.

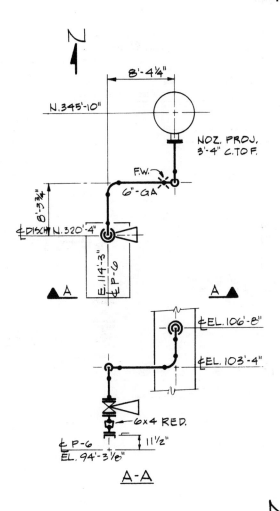

N

8'-4¼"

N. 345'-10"

NOZ. PROJ.
3'-4" C. TO F.

F.W.

6"-GA

8'-3¾"

℄ DISCH N. 320'-4"

E. 114'-3"
℄ P-6

▲A   A▲

℄ EL. 106'-8"

℄ EL. 103'-4"

6x4 RED.

℄ P-6
EL. 94'-3⅛"   11½"

A-A

Isometric Sketch of Fig. Prob. 8-2A

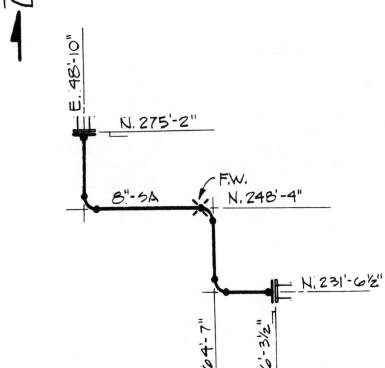

N

E. 48'-10"

N. 275'-2"

F.W.
N. 248'-4"

8"-5A

N. 231'-6½"

E. 64'-7"

E. 76'-3½"

Isometric Sketch of Fig. Prob. 8-2B

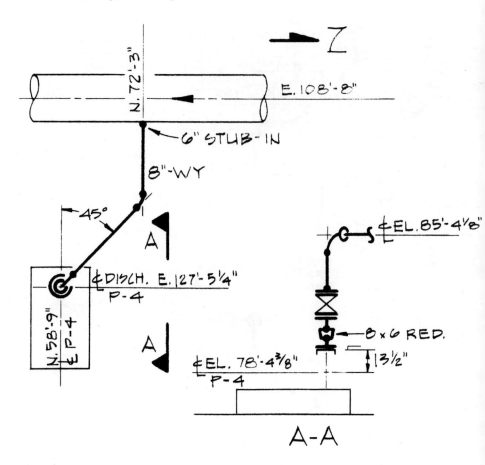

N. 72'-3"

E. 108'-8"

6" STUB-IN

8"-WY

45°

A

¢ DISCH. E. 127'-5¼"
P-4

A

N. 58'-9"
¢ P-4

¢ EL. 85'-4⅛"

8 x 6 RED.

3½"

¢ EL. 78'-4⅜"
P-4

A-A

Isometric Sketch of Prob. 8-2C

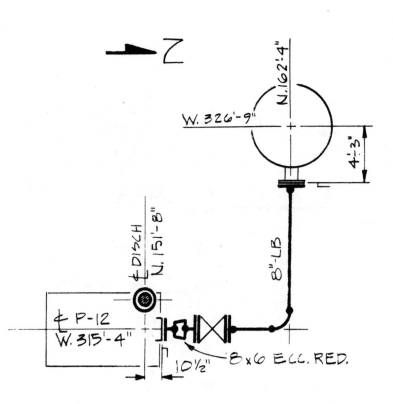

N. 162'-4"

W. 326'-9"

4'-3"

8"-LB

¢ DISCH
N. 151'-8"

¢ P-12
W. 315'-4"

10½"

8 x 6 ECC. RED.

Isometric Sketch of Fig. Prob. 8-2D

Fig. Prob. 8-2 (continued)

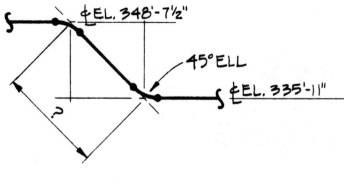

ANSWER _____

Fig. Prob. 8-5A

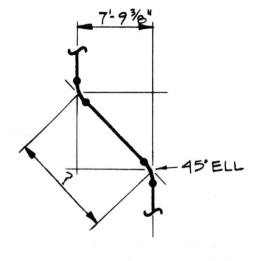

ANSWER _____

Fig. Prob. 8-5B

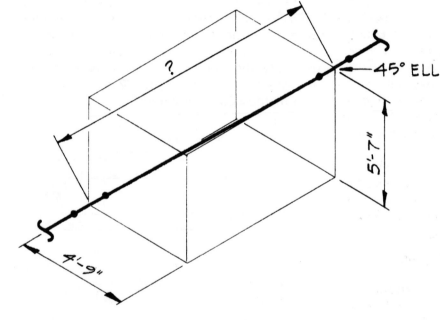

ANSWER _____

Fig. Prob. 8-5C

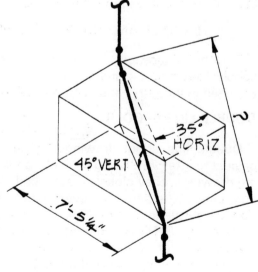

ANSWER _____

Fig. Prob. 8-5D

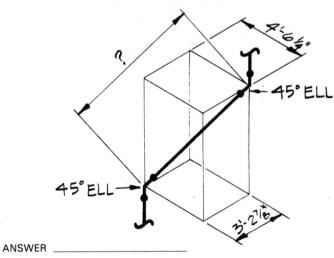

ANSWER _____

Fig. Prob. 8-5E

Fig. Prob. 8-5

Chapter 9

PIPING SPOOLS

A SPOOL to a drafter or pipefitter is an assembly of pipe and fittings that can be welded in the shop in less time (and for less pay) than it would take to weld in the field (at the construction site). Hence, a spool drawing is the last in a series of drawings before the final torch is lit. It basically is a subassembly drawing that will be crumpled, folded, and soiled by the working hands of welders and pipefitters. It becomes *their* shop drawing; their instructions.

Creation of spool drawings is often done by the contractor. On occasion, they may be done by the engineering firm, job shoppers, or free-lancers. "Spools" are simple drawings, but important ones. Let's take a look at how they're made.

LAYOUT AND CONSTRUCTION

Two basic methods are used to illustrate pipe spools: the single line and double line methods. Both are used in industry, and each has its advantages.

DOUBLE LINE SPOOLS

Double line spool drawings probably are the easiest to interpret. Being basically double line piping drawings, they closely resemble the actual appearance of the pipe. However, double line spools do take a little longer to draw than the single line version. Fig. 9-1 is an example of the orthographic layout used for double line spools.

When creating a spool drawing, you should try to show the shape of the entire spool in one view. Only if this is impossible should you resort to extra views. Note the use of centerlines and hidden lines in Fig. 9-1. Always begin your layout with centerlines. Draw the skeleton, then add the skin. Add dimensions later.

SINGLE LINE SPOOLS

Single line spool drawings take less time and are easier to draw, but they do require some visualiza-

tion skills for the drafter as well as for the pipefitter who reads them. The centerline becomes the pipe, and it is drawn as a heavy line. Centerline extensions are shown at elbows and flanges. Again, use only the number of views required to fully describe the assembly. Fig. 9-2 is a single line version of the spool shown in Fig. 9-1.

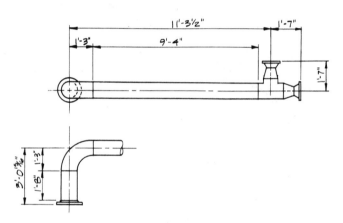

Fig. 9-1. Orthographic layout of a double line pipe spool drawing.

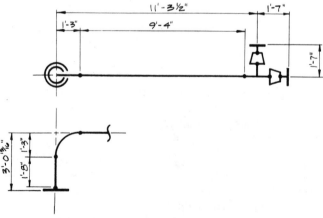

Fig. 9-2. Orthographic layout of a single line pipe spool drawing.

Companies wishing to keep drafting time to a minimum while maintaining an easily interpreted drawing resort to the "single-double" (hybrid or half-breed) method. You guessed it. The pipe is shown in single line, and the fittings are drawn double line. An example is shown in Fig. 9-3.

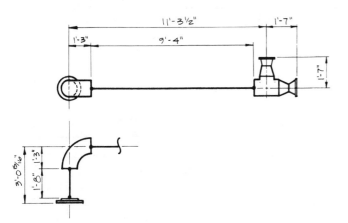

Fig. 9-3. Single-double method of pipe spool representation. Note single line pipe and double line fittings.

SCALES AND SIZE

How much pipe should be shown on the spool drawing? This is a question often asked by beginning drafters. Listen up. The size of the pipe spool is normally determined by the dimensions of the conveyance the contractor will use. How big is the contractor's truck? The spools must be hauled from the shop to the construction site, so they can only be so big. If you know the size of the truck or rail car, you can easily calculate the spool size from the isometric drawing. Remember, you're dealing with three dimensions.

Keep in mind that valves are not shown in spool drawings. They are installed in the field. Knowing this often eliminates some decisions about where to break spools.

Spools must also be tagged with identification numbers. Companies vary on the marking method, but a common one uses the pipe specification plus an additional number or letter to identify the spool. These "marks" or "tag numbers" usually are first shown on the isometric drawing. Fig. 8-3 is a good example. These numbers are also spray painted on the spool itself for identification during erection.

Scale is often "thrown to the wind" on spool drawings. Some companies prefer not to use a scale and totally rely on written dimensions. This makes it easy and fast to draw spools with a computer aided drafting system. Other companies draw the

spools at a certain scale, depending on the size of the spool and the pipe diameter. The no-scale method is quick, and it is often used by contractors concerned with cutting costs. In both cases, written dimensions are the "sacred cows" of these drawings. These *must* be accurate. Check dimensions two or three times.

DIMENSIONING SPOOLS

Spools can be dimensioned by using a couple of variations on a theme. Two common methods are shown in examples A and B in Fig. 9-4. Regardless of the method used, it is always important to know the exact lengths of pipe and the locations of any branches. These are critical. However, most companies involved in spooling often include a few in-

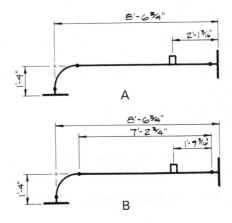

Fig. 9-4. Two acceptable pipe spool dimensioning methods. Study differences at A and B.

ches extra in the dimensions for straight pipe. This hopefully covers any miscalculations or mistakes.

BILL OF MATERIALS

The BILL OF MATERIALS (B.O.M.) is the material list of the spool drawing. It contains the vital statistics of all ingredients needed to create the spool. When this type of drawing is done on some CADD systems, all of the pipe and fittings are automatically tabulated as you draw. The B.O.M. is then generated by the computer without additional calculations by the drafter.

ITEM NUMBERS

ITEM NUMBERS serve to identify a piece of pipe or a fitting on the drawing and key it to a description in the B.O.M. The item number is often found

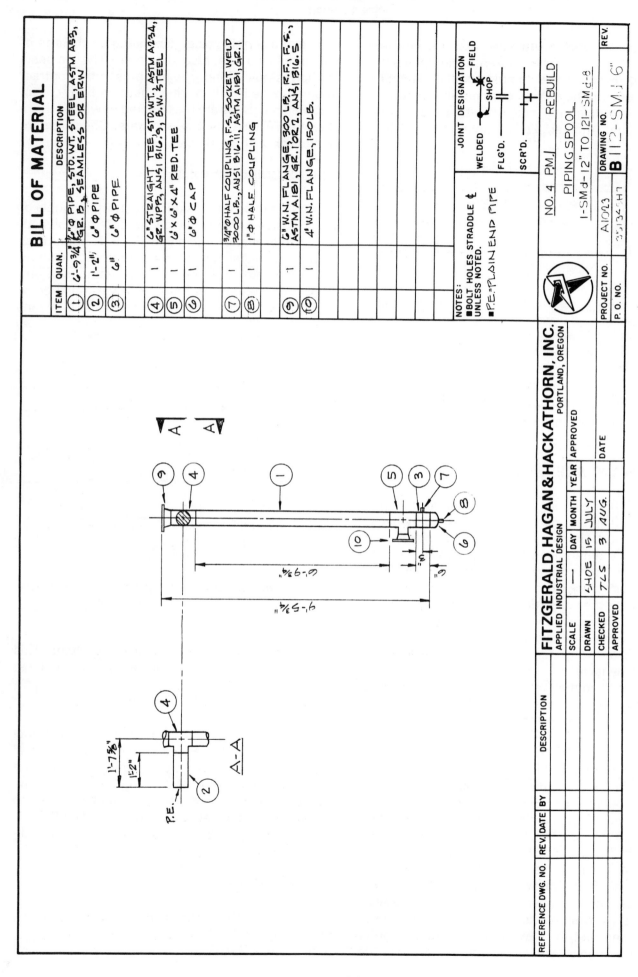

Fig. 9-5. Example of Bill of Material found on an industry spool drawing. (Fitzgerald, Hagan & Hackathorn, Inc.)

inside a circle on the drawing with a leader line pointing to the part. The same number appears in the bill of materials, and it is followed by a detailed description of the part. Fig. 9-5 contains examples of item numbers.

MATERIAL DESCRIPTION

The MATERIAL DESCRIPTION can be handled in one column or it may be broken down into ''quantity'' and ''description.'' A detailed description of the material *is* required. This information may be used by pipefitters, purchasing agents, and cost estimators. The bill of materials in Fig. 9-5 shows the order in which the pipe and fittings are listed. A common method is to show pipe (lowest schedule number and smallest diameter first), then common fittings, then flanges and, finally, odd fittings. Often the last two categories are reversed. Also, some companies may list pipe last.

Always remember the purpose of spool drawings and the requirements of the people using them. With this in mind, be certain that your dimensions are accurate and that the information within the bill of materials is complete.

SUMMARY

The purpose of PROCESS PIPE DRAFTING has been to introduce you to the basic concepts and techniques inherent in piping drafting. This text has made no attempts to teach design of piping systems. That subject is covered thoroughly in other books.

You, the drafter, should keep in mind that your primary responsibility is to create an accurate, well laid out, easily read piping drawing. As a junior drafter, constructing a drawing from sketches, notes, vendor drawings, and verbal descriptions will be your job and, hopefully, this text will aid you in that task.

Pipe drafters eventually assume greater responsibilities and find themselves designing piping arrangements, calculating bends and offsets, locating equipment, etc. These are challenging duties and most of them cannot be taught completely in a book. The best teacher is experience on the job. The quirks and exceptions of piping become glaringly obvious to the drafter working at the job site searching for the elusive pipe.

Process pipe drafting is an interesting field, and there's always room for good ''pipers.'' Enjoy your piping.

REVIEW QUESTIONS

1. Who uses the spool drawing? _____
   _____

2. List the three methods of drawing pipe spools and briefly state the characteristics of each.

   a. _____
   _____
   _____
   _____

   b. _____
   _____
   _____
   _____

   c. _____
   _____
   _____
   _____

3. How big are pipe spools? _____
   _____
   _____

4. What is the most common scale used on spool drawings? _____
   _____

5. Why is extra pipe often included on spool drawings? _____
   _____

6. What is the B.O.M.? _____
   _____
   _____
   _____

7. What is a good order to list items in the B.O.M.? _____
   _____
   _____
   _____
   _____
   _____

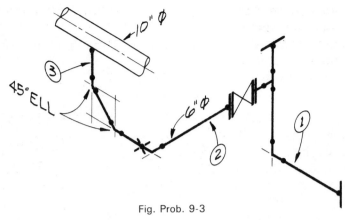

Fig. Prob. 9-3

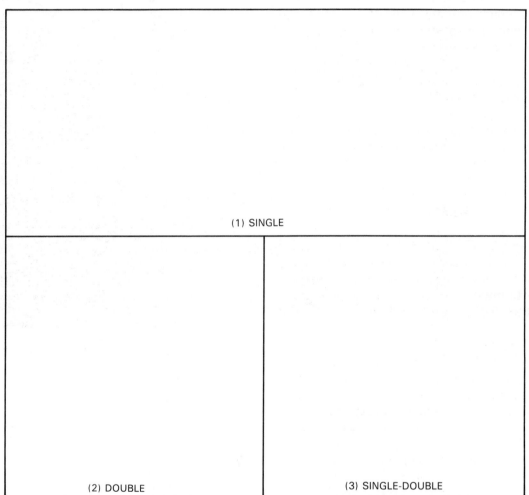

(1) SINGLE

(2) DOUBLE

(3) SINGLE-DOUBLE

PROBLEMS

PROB. 9-1. Redraw the three spools shown isometrically in Fig. 8-3 as single line and double line orthographic spools. Create a bill of material for each.

PROB. 9-2. Redraw the orthographic spool in Fig. 9-2 as an isometric. Fully dimension your drawing. Use proper isometric lettering.

PROB. 9-3. Create a spool drawing of each of the three spools indicated in Fig. Prob. 9-3. Use the methods indicated in the spaces provided for your drawings. Your instructor will decide if drawings are to be done with a straight edge or freehand.

PROB. 9-4. Create a spool drawing for each of the spools in Prob. 9-3 on B size vellum. Your instructor will assign diameter and dimensions to the straight lengths of pipe. Flanges to be 150#, gaskets 1/16'' thick. Construct a bill of material for each spool.

PROB. 9-5. Draw the necessary spools for each problem in Fig. Prob. 8-2. Be aware of the field welds and valves. Use either single or double line. Use B size vellum. Construct a bill of material for each spool.

Pipefitters use spool drawings to construct piping runs such as this insulated steam piping system at a paper mill. (Weyerhaeuser Co.)

APPENDIX A
ABBREVIATIONS

This appendix presents common abbreviations used within the process piping industry and related fields. Refer to it often. Become familiar with as many abbreviations as you can. Learn what they stand for; you will see a lot of them on piping drawings.

A

AB / Anchor bolt
AISI / American Iron and Steel Institute
ANSI / American National Standards Institute
API / American Petroleum Institute
APP'D / Approved
ARRG'T / Arrangement
ASME / American Society of
      Mechanical Engineers
ASSY / Assembly
ASTM / American Society for Testing
      and Materials
AUX / Auxiliary
AVG / Average
AWS / American Welding Society

B

BL / Bay line
BC / Bolt circle or between centers
BE / Beveled end
BEV / Bevel
BF (B'FLG) / Blind Flange
BF / Bronze fitted
BL / Bottom level
BLDG / Building
BOC / Bottom of conduit
BOM (B/M) / Bill of Material
BOP / Bottom of pipe
BOT / Bottom
BRKT / Bracket
BRS / Brass
BW / Buttweld

C

C / Channel steel
C to F / Center to face
CFM / Cubic feet per minute
CHG / Change
CI / Cast Iron
CO / Chain operator or clean out
CON / Concentric
CONC / Concrete
COND / Condensate
CONN / Connection
CONST JT / Construction joint
CONT / Continue
CONTR / Contractor
CONVR / Conveyor

CPLG / Coupling
CRS / Cold rolled steel
CS / Carbon steel or cold spring
CU FT / Cubic foot
CU IN / Cubic inch
CU YD / Cubic yard
CYL / Cylinder

D

DBL / Double
DEPT / Department
DET / Detail
DIA (ϕ) / Diameter
DIM / Dimension
DISCH / Discharge
DP / Drip proof
DSGN / Design
DWG / Drawing

E

EA / Each
ECC / Eccentric
E-E / End to end
EL / Elevation
ELEC / Electric
ELEV / Elevation
ELL / Elbow
EMER / Emergency
ENGR / Engineer
EQUIP / Equipment
ERW / Electric resistance weld
EST / Estimate
EVAP / Evaporator
EXH / Exhaust
EXIST / Existing
EXP JT / Expansion Joint
EXT / Extension

F

FAB / Fabricate
FD / Floor Drain
FDN / Foundation
FEM / Female
F / Fahrenheit
F-F / Face to face
FH / Fixed hanger
FIG / Figure
FIN / Finish

FL / Floor
FLEX / Flexible
FLG / Flange
FOB / Flat on bottom
FOT / Flat on top
FRP / Fiberglass reinforced pipe
FS / Forged steel
FT / Foot (feet)
FTG / Fitting, footing
FT LB / Foot pounds
FW / Field weld

G

GA / Gage
GALV / Galvanize
GALV STL / Galvanized steel
GEN / General
GEN ARRG'T / General arrangement
GPH / Gallons per hour
GPM / Gallons per minute
GRD / Grade
GRND / Ground
GSKT / Gasket
GV / Gate valve

H

HD / Head
HDR / Header
HEX / Hexagon
HGT / Height
HI PRESS / High pressure
HORIZ / Horizontal
HP / Horsepower
HS / High speed
HTR / Heater
HVY / Heavy

I

ID / Inside diameter
IE / Invert elevation
IND / Indicate
INS / Insulate
INSP / Inspect
INST / Instrument
INSTL / Install
INV / Invert
IP / Iron pipe
IPS / Iron pipe size
ISO / Isometric

J

JCT / Junction
JT / Joint

K

K / Kip (1000 lb)
KD / Kiln dried
KW / Kilowatt

L

L / Angle steel
LAB / Laboratory
LBR / Lumber
LG / Long
LGTH / Length
LH / Left hand
LIN / Lineal
LIQ / Liquor
LP / Low pressure or Low point
LR / Long radius
LTD / Limited
LUB / Lubricate

M

MACH / Machine
MAT'L / Material
MAX / Maximum
MCC / Motor control center
MECH / Mechanical
MED / Medium
MFG / Manufacturing
MH / Manhole
MI / Malleable iron
MS / Mild steel
MTG / Mounting
MTR / Motor

N

NC / Normally closed
NIP / Nipple
NO / Normally open
NOM / Nominal
NOZ / Nozzle
NPS / Nominal pipe size
NPT / National pipe thread
NTS / Not to scale

O

OAL / Overall length
OD / Outside diameter
OLT / Outlet
O-O / Out to out
OPNG / Opening
OPP / Opposite
ORIF / Orifice
OSHA / Occupational Safety & Health
        Administration

P

PE / Plain end
PED / Pedestal
PERM / Permanent
PERP / Perpendicular
PL / Plate
PNEU / Pneumatic
PNL / Panel

POE / Plain one end
PRESS / Pressure
PROJ / Project or projection
PRV / Pressure relief valve
PS / Pipe support
PSI / Pounds per square inch
PSIG / Pounds per square inch gage
PT / Point

R

REC / Recirculate
RED / Reducer
REF / Reference
REINF / Reinforce
REQD / Required
RET / Return
REV / Revision
RF / Raised face
RPM / Revolutions per minute

S

SCH / Schedule
SCRD / Screwed
SCRN / Screen
SHT / Sheet
S'LET / Sockolet
SOC / Socket
SO FLG / Slip on flange
SPEC / Specification
SR / Short radius
SS / Stainless steel
STA / Station
STD / Standard
STM / Steam
STL / Steel
SUCT / Suction
SUP / Support
SW / Socket weld
SYM / Symmetrical
SYS / System

T

TBE / Thread both ends

TE / Threaded end
TEMP / Temperature
TERM / Terminal
THD / Thread
THRU / Through
TIP / Tie in point
TK / Tank
TL / Top level
T'LET / Threadolet
TOC / Top of concrete, top of conduit
TOE / Thread one end
TOG / Top of grating
TOP / Top of pipe
TOS / Top of steel
TRC / Top of rough concrete
TURB / Turbine
TYP / Typical

V

VAC / Vacuum
VAR / Variable
VEL / Velocity
VERT / Vertical
VISC / Viscosity
VLE / Valve
VOL / Volume

W

W / Wide flange steel shape
W/ / With
WI / Wrought iron
WN FLG / Weld neck flange
W'LET / Weldolet
WOG / Water oil and gas
WP / Working point

X

XFMR / Transformer
XH / Extra heavy
XMTR / Transmitter
XS / Extra strong
XXS / Double extra strong

This appendix provides two comprehensive charts of welded fitting and flange specifications. The information contained in these charts is useful when drawing fittings and flanges to scale, and when calculating pipe and fitting assemblies.

The first chart gives specifications for Seamless Welded Fittings. The second chart covers ANSI Forged Steel Flanges. All specifications are coded to nominal pipe size (NPS).

To use the Seamless Welded Fittings chart, first find the nominal pipe size of the fitting required, then look for the letter that represents the dimension you need. Your answer will be at the intersection of these two columns.

NOTE: When working with reducers and reducing tees, always use the large end of the fitting as nominal pipe size.

The ANSI Forged Steel Flanges chart gives various key dimensions for 150-2500 lb. flanges and welding neck flange bores. When working with this chart, use the same method of locating a needed dimension as you employed with the fittings chart. First find the NPS of the flange required, then look for the letter or chart heading that represents the dimension you need. Again, your answer will be at the intersection of these two columns.

Following are examples of how to use the charts to find the dimension you need.

Example A: Seamless Welded Fittings Chart

Find the "A" dimension for a 6 in. diameter, 90° long radius elbow.
1. Locate "6" in Nom. Pipe Size column on right side of table.
2. Find large letter "A" along top of chart.
3. Find intersection of these two. Dimension should be 9 in.

Example B: Seamless Welded Fittings Chart

Find the inside diameter (I.D.) of an 8 in. diameter pipe with a wall thickness rating of "Sch. 80."
1. Locate "8" in Nom. Pipe Size column on left side of table.
2. Find "Sch 80" column under WALL THICKNESS heading.
3. Find intersection of these two numbers. Wall thickness should be .500 in.
4. Multiply this number by two: .500 x 2 = 1.000.
5. Under "Pipe O.D." column, find size for an 8 in. N.P.S. pipe. It should be 8.625.
6. Subtract total wall thicknesses (1.00) from 8.625. I.D. of 8 in. diameter schedule 80 pipe should be 7.625. This is a good example of why 8 in. diameter designation is a "nominal pipe size" (commercial designation).

Example C: ANSI Forged Steel Flanges Chart

Find the "Y" dimension for a 12 in. diameter welding neck flange with a rating of 300 lbs.
1. Locate "12" in Nom. Pipe Size column on chart.
2. Find "Weld Neck" column under 300 LB. FLANGES heading at top of chart.
3. Find intersection of these two variables. Your answer should be 5 1/8".

Example D: ANSI Forged Steel Flanges Chart

Find the "O" dimension of an 18 in. N.P.S. 600 lb. S.O. flange.
1. Locate "O" column under 600 LB. FLANGES heading in middle of chart.
2. Find "18" in Nom. Pipe Size column on left side of chart.
3. Find intersection of these two numbers. Your answer should be 29 1/4 in.

Seamless Welding Fittings

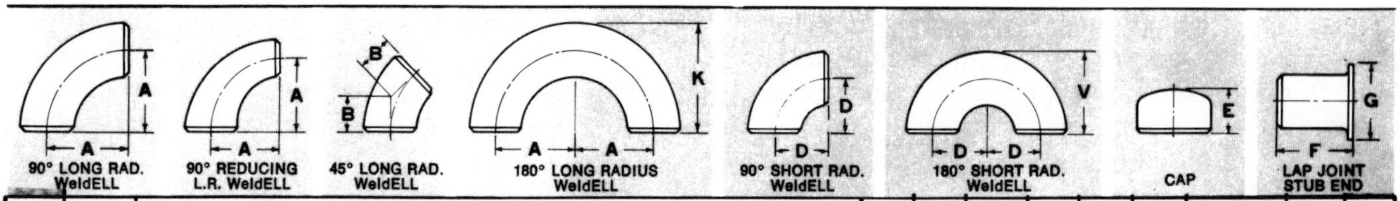
A
A
90° LONG RAD. WeldELL
A
A
90° REDUCING L.R. WeldELL
B
B
45° LONG RAD. WeldELL
K
A
A
180° LONG RADIUS WeldELL
D
D
90° SHORT RAD. WeldELL
V
D
D
180° SHORT RAD. WeldELL
E
CAP
G
F
LAP JOINT STUB END

Nom. Pipe Size	Pipe O.D.	① Light Wall	Sch 20	Sch 30	② Std	Sch 40	Sch 60	③ X-Stg	Sch 80	Sch 100	Sch 120	Sch 140	Sch 160	XX-Stg	A	B	K	D	V	⑦ E	F ASA	F MSS	G	Nom. Pipe Size
½	.840	.083	...	...	.109	.109	...	.147	.147	...	...	...	.188	.294	1½	⅝	1⅞	...	...	1	3	2	1⅜	½
¾	1.050	.083	...	...	.113	.113	...	.154	.154	...	...	...	.219	.308	1⅛	7/16	1 11/16	...	...	1	3	2	1 11/16	¾
1	1.315	.109	...	...	.133	.133	...	.179	.179	...	...	...	.250	.358	1½	⅞	2 3/16	1	1⅝	1½	4	2	2	1
1¼	1.660	.109	...	...	.140	.140	...	.191	.191	...	...	...	.250	.382	1⅞	1	2¾	1¼	2 1/16	1½	4	2	2½	1¼
1½	1.900	.109	...	...	.145	.145	...	.200	.200	...	...	...	.281	.400	2¼	1⅛	3¼	1½	2 7/16	1½	4	2	2⅞	1½
2	2.375	.109	...	...	.154	.154	...	.218	.218	...	...	...	.344	.436	3	1⅜	4 3/16	2	3 3/16	1½	6	2½	3⅝	2
2½	2.875	.120	...	...	.203	.203	...	.276	.276	...	...	...	.375	.552	3¾	1¾	5 3/16	2½	3 15/16	1½	6	2½	4⅛	2½
3	3.500	.120	...	...	.216	.216	...	.300	.300	...	...	...	.438	.600	4½	2	6¼	3	4¾	2	6	2½	5	3
3½	4.000	.120	...	...	.226	.226	...	.318	.318	...	...	...	...	.636	5¼	2¼	7¼	3½	5½	2½	6	3	5½	3½
4	4.500	.120	...	...	.237	.237	...	.337	.337	...	.438	...	.531	.674	6	2½	8¼	4	6¼	2½	6	3	6 3/16	4
5	5.563	.134	...	...	.258	.258	...	.375	.375	...	.500	...	.625	.750	7½	3⅛	10 5/16	5	7¾	3	8	3	7 5/16	5
6	6.625	.134	...	...	.280	.280	...	.432	.432	...	.562	...	.719	.864	9	3¾	12 5/16	6	9 5/16	3½	8	3½	8½	6
8	8.625	.148	.250	.277	.322	.322	.406	.500	.500	.594	.719	.812	.906	.875	12	5	16 5/16	8	12 5/16	4	8	4	10⅝	8
10	10.750	.165	.250	.307	.365	.365	.500	.500	.594	.719	.844	1.000	1.125	1.000	15	6¼	20⅜	10	15⅜	5	10	5	12¾	10
12	12.750	.180	.250	.330	.375	.406	.562	.500	.688	.844	1.000	1.125	1.312	1.000	18	7½	24⅜	12	18⅜	6	10	6	15	12
14	14.000	.250	.312	.375	.375	.438	.594	.500	.750	.938	1.094	1.250	1.406	...	21	8¾	28	14	21	6½	12	...	16¼	14
16	16.000	.250	.312	.375	.375	.500	.656	.500	.844	1.031	1.219	1.438	1.594	...	24	10	32	16	24	7	12	...	18½	16
18	18.000	.250	.312	.438	.375	.562	.750	.500	.938	1.156	1.375	1.562	1.781	...	27	11¼	36	18	27	8	12	...	21	18
20	20.000	.250	.375	.500	.375	.594	.812	.500	1.031	1.281	1.500	1.750	1.969	...	30	12½	40	20	30	9	12	...	23	20
24	24.000	.250	.375	.562	.375	.688	.969	.500	1.219	1.531	1.812	2.062	2.344	...	36	15	48	24	36	10½	12	...	27¼	24
30	30.000	.312	.500	.625	.375	...	...	.500	...	...	...	...	...	...	45	18½	60	30	45	10½	...	...	...	30
36 ④	36.000	.312	.500	.625	.375	.750	...	.500	...	...	...	...	...	...	54	22¼	...	36	54	10½	...	...	...	36 ④
42 ④	42.000	...	...	...	.375	...	...	.500	...	...	...	...	...	...	63	26	...	42	...	12	...	...	...	42 ④
48 ④	48.000	...	...	...	.375	...	...	.500	...	...	...	...	...	...	72	29¾	...	48	...	13½	...	...	...	48 ④

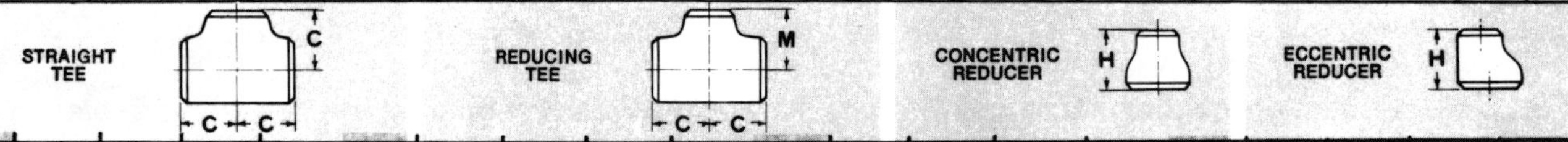
STRAIGHT TEE
C
C
C
REDUCING TEE
M
C
C
CONCENTRIC REDUCER
H
ECCENTRIC REDUCER
H

Nom. Pipe Size	Outlet	C	M	H
¾	¾	1⅛	...	...
	½	1⅛	1⅛	1½
1	1	1½	...	...
	¾	1½	1½	2
	½	1½	1½	2
1¼	1¼	1⅞	...	...
	1	1⅞	1⅞	2
	¾	1⅞	1⅞	2
	½	1⅞	1⅞	2
1½	1½	2¼	...	...
	1¼	2¼	2¼	2½
	1	2¼	2¼	2½
	¾	2¼	2¼	2½
	½	2¼	2¼	2½
2	2	2½	...	...
	1½	2½	2⅜	3
	1¼	2½	2¼	3
	1	2½	2	3
	¾	2½	1¾	3
2½	2½	3	...	...
	2	3	2¾	3½
	1½	3	2⅝	3½
	1¼	3	2½	3½
	1	3	2¼	3½
3	3	3⅜	...	...
	2½	3⅜	3¼	3½
	2	3⅜	3	3½
	1½	3⅜	2⅞	3½
	1¼	3⅜	2¾	3½

Nom. Pipe Size	Outlet	C	M	H
3½	3½	3¾	...	...
	3	3¾	3⅝	4
	2½	3¾	3½	4
	2	3¾	3¼	4
	1½	3¾	3⅛	4
4	4	4⅛	...	...
	3½	4⅛	4	4
	3	4⅛	3⅞	4
	2½	4⅛	3¾	4
	2	4⅛	3½	4
	1½	4⅛	3⅜	4
5	5	4⅞	...	...
	4	4⅞	4⅝	5
	3½	4⅞	4½	5
	3	4⅞	4⅜	5
	2½	4⅞	4¼	5
	2	4⅞	4⅛	5
6	6	5⅝	...	...
	5	5⅝	5⅜	5½
	4	5⅝	5⅛	5½
	3½	5⅝	5	5½
	3	5⅝	4⅞	5½
	2½	5⅝	4¾	5½
8	8	7	...	...
	6	7	6⅝	6
	5	7	6⅜	6
	4	7	6⅛	6
	3½	7	6	6

Nom. Pipe Size	Outlet	C	M	H
10	10	8½	...	...
	8	8½	8	7
	6	8½	7⅝	7
	5	8½	7½	7
	4	8½	7¼	7
12	12	10	...	...
	10	10	9½	8
	8	10	9	8
	6	10	8⅝	8
	5	10	8½	8
14	14	11	...	...
	12	11	10⅝	13
	10	11	10⅛	13
	8	11	9¾	13
	6	11	9⅜	13
16	16	12	...	...
	14	12	12	14
	12	12	11⅝	14
	10	12	11⅛	14
	8	12	10¾	14
	6	12	10⅜	14
18	18	13½	...	...
	16	13½	13	15
	14	13½	13	15
	12	13½	12⅝	15
	10	13½	12⅛	15
	8	13½	11¾	15

Nom. Pipe Size	Outlet	C	M	H
20	20	15	...	...
	18	15	14½	20
	16	15	14	20
	14	15	14	20
	12	15	13⅝	20
	10	15	13⅛	20
	8	15	12¾	20
24 ④	24	17	...	...
	20	17	17	20
	18	17	16½	20
	16	17	16	20
	14	17	16	20
	12	17	15⅝	20
	10	17	15⅛	20
30 ④	30	22	...	...
	24	22	21	24
	20	22	20	24
	18	22	19½	24
	16	22	19	24
	14	22	19	24
36 ④	36	26½	...	...
	30	26½	25	24
	24	26½	24	24
	20	26½	23	24
	18	26½	22½	24
	16	26½	22	24
42 ④	42	30	28	...
	36	30	28	24
	30	30	28	24
	24	30	26	24
	20	30	26	24
48	48	35	33	...
	42	35	32	28
	36	35	31	28
	30	35	30	28

NOTES:
① Light Wall thicknesses are identical to stainless steel Schedule 10S in sizes thru 12", and to Schedule 10 in sizes 14" and larger.
② Standard Wall thicknesses are identical to stainless steel Schedule 40S in sizes thru 12".
③ Extra Strong Wall thicknesses are identical to stainless steel Schedule 80S in sizes thru 12".
④ May be of welded pipe, x-rayed and stress-relieved.
⑤ Other types, sizes and thicknesses of fittings on application.
⑥ Stocked in carbon steel and a variety of other metals and alloys.
⑦ See ANSI B16.9 for cap lengths when wall thicknesses are greater than x-stg.

Fig. B-1. Chart of Seamless Welding Fittings (Taylor-Bonney Div., Gulf + Western Mfg. Co.)

ANSI Forged Steel Flanges

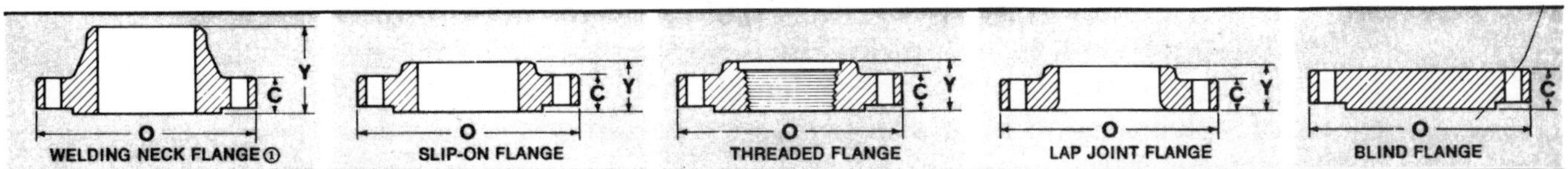

150 LB. FLANGES

Nom. Pipe Size	O	C②	Y② Weld Neck	Y② Slip on Thrd.	Y② Lap Joint	Bolt Circle	No. and Size of Holes
½	3½	7/16	1⅞	⅝	⅝	2⅜	4-⅝
¾	3⅞	½	2 1/16	⅝	⅝	2¾	4-⅝
1	4¼	9/16	2 3/16	11/16	11/16	3⅛	4-⅝
1¼	4⅝	⅝	2¼	13/16	13/16	3½	4-⅝
1½	5	11/16	2 7/16	⅞	⅞	3⅞	4-⅝
2	6	¾	2½	1	1	4¾	4-¾
2½	7	⅞	2¾	1⅛	1⅛	5½	4-¾
3	7½	15/16	2¾	1 3/16	1 3/16	6	4-¾
3½	8½	15/16	2 13/16	1¼	1¼	7	8-¾
4	9	15/16	3	1 5/16	1 5/16	7½	8-¾
5	10	15/16	3½	1 7/16	1 7/16	8½	8-⅞
6	11	1	3½	1 9/16	1 9/16	9½	8-⅞
8	13½	1⅛	4	1¾	1¾	11¾	8-⅞
10	16	1 3/16	4	1 15/16	1 15/16	14¼	12-1
12	19	1¼	4½	2 3/16	2 3/16	17	12-1
14	21	1⅜	5	2¼	3⅛	18¾	12-1⅛
16	23½	1 7/16	5	2½	3 7/16	21¼	16-1⅛
18	25	1 9/16	5½	2 11/16	3 13/16	22¾	16-1¼
20	27½	1 11/16	5 11/16	2⅞	4 1/16	25	20-1¼
24	32	1⅞	6	3¼	4⅜	29½	20-1⅜

300 LB. FLANGES

Nom. Pipe Size	O	C②	Y② Weld Neck	Y② Slip on Thrd.	Y② Lap Joint	Bolt Circle	No. and Size of Holes
½	3¾	9/16	2 1/16	⅞	⅞	2⅝	4-⅝
¾	4⅝	⅝	2¼	1	1	3¼	4-¾
1	4⅞	11/16	2 7/16	1 1/16	1 1/16	3½	4-¾
1¼	5¼	¾	2 9/16	1 1/16	1 1/16	3⅞	4-¾
1½	6⅛	13/16	2 11/16	1 3/16	1 3/16	4½	4-⅞
2	6½	⅞	2¾	1 5/16	1 5/16	5	8-¾
2½	7½	1	3	1½	1½	5⅞	8-⅞
3	8¼	1⅛	3⅛	1 11/16	1 11/16	6⅝	8-⅞
3½	9	1 3/16	3 3/16	1¾	1¾	7¼	8-⅞
4	10	1¼	3⅜	1⅞	1⅞	7⅞	8-⅞
5	11	1⅜	3⅞	2	2	9¼	8-⅞
6	12½	1 7/16	3⅞	2 1/16	2 1/16	10⅝	12-⅞
8	15	1⅝	4⅜	2 7/16	2 7/16	13	12-1
10	17½	1⅞	4⅝	2⅝	3¾	15¼	16-1⅛
12	20½	2	5⅛	2⅞	4	17¾	16-1¼
14	23	2⅛	5⅝	3	4⅜	20¼	20-1¼
16	25½	2¼	5¾	3¼	4¾	22½	20-1⅜
18	28	2⅜	6¼	3½	5⅛	24¾	24-1⅜
20	30½	2½	6⅜	3¾	5½	27	24-1⅜
24	36	2¾	6⅝	4 3/16	6	32	24-1⅝

400 LB. FLANGES

Nom. Pipe Size	O	C②	Y② Weld Neck	Y② Slip on Thrd.	Y② Lap Joint	Bolt Circle	No. and Size of Holes
½	3¾	9/16	2 1/16	⅞	⅞	2⅝	4-⅝
¾	4⅝	⅝	2¼	1	1	3¼	4-¾
1	4⅞	11/16	2 7/16	1 1/16	1 1/16	3½	4-¾
1¼	5¼	13/16	2⅝	1⅛	1⅛	3⅞	4-¾
1½	6⅛	⅞	2¾	1¼	1¼	4½	4-⅞
2	6½	1	2⅞	1 7/16	1 7/16	5	8-¾
2½	7½	1⅛	3⅛	1⅝	1⅝	5⅞	8-⅞
3	8¼	1¼	3¼	1 13/16	1 13/16	6⅝	8-⅞
3½	9	1⅜	3⅜	1 15/16	1 15/16	7¼	8-1
4	10	1⅜	3½	2	2	7⅞	8-1
5	11	1½	4	2⅛	2⅛	9¼	8-1
6	12½	1⅝	4 1/16	2¼	2¼	10⅝	12-1
8	15	1⅞	4⅝	2 11/16	2 11/16	13	12-1⅛
10	17½	2⅛	4⅞	2⅞	4	15¼	16-1¼
12	20½	2¼	5⅜	3⅛	4¼	17¾	16-1⅜
14	23	2⅜	5⅞	3 5/16	4⅝	20¼	20-1⅜
16	25½	2½	6	3 11/16	5	22½	20-1½
18	28	2⅝	6½	3⅞	5⅜	24¾	24-1½
20	30½	2¾	6⅝	4	5¾	27	24-1⅝
24	36	3	6⅞	4½	6¼	32	24-1⅞

600 LB. FLANGES

Nom. Pipe Size	O	C②	Y② Weld Neck	Y② Slip on Thrd.	Y② Lap Joint	Bolt Circle	No. and Size of Holes
½	3¾	9/16	2 1/16	⅞	⅞	2⅝	4-⅝
¾	4⅝	⅝	2¼	1	1	3¼	4-¾
1	4⅞	11/16	2 7/16	1 1/16	1 1/16	3½	4-¾
1¼	5¼	13/16	2⅝	1⅛	1⅛	3⅞	4-¾
1½	6⅛	⅞	2¾	1¼	1¼	4½	4-⅞
2	6½	1	2⅞	1 7/16	1 7/16	5	8-¾
2½	7½	1⅛	3⅛	1⅝	1⅝	5⅞	8-⅞
3	8¼	1¼	3¼	1 13/16	1 13/16	6⅝	8-⅞
3½	9	1⅜	3⅜	1 15/16	1 15/16	7¼	8-1
4	10¾	1½	4	2⅛	2⅛	8½	8-1
5	13	1¾	4½	2⅜	2⅜	10½	8-1⅛
6	14	1⅞	4⅝	2⅝	2⅝	11½	12-1⅛
8	16½	2 3/16	5¼	3	3	13¾	12-1¼
10	20	2½	6	3⅜	4⅜	17	16-1⅜
12	22	2⅝	6⅛	3⅝	4⅝	19¼	20-1⅜
14	23¾	2¾	6½	3 11/16	5	20¾	20-1½
16	27	3	7	4 3/16	5½	23¾	20-1⅝
18	29¼	3¼	7¼	4⅝	6	25¾	20-1¾
20	32	3½	7½	5	6½	28½	24-1¾
24	37	4	8	5½	7¼	33	24-2

900 LB. FLANGES

Nom. Pipe Size	O	C②	Y② Weld Neck	Y② Slip on Thrd.	Y② Lap Joint	Bolt Circle	No. and Size of Holes
½	4¾	⅞	2⅜	1¼	1¼	3¼	4-⅞
¾	5⅛	1	2¾	1⅜	1⅜	3½	4-⅞
1	5⅞	1⅛	2⅞	1⅝	1⅝	4	4-1
1¼	6¼	1⅛	2⅞	1⅝	1⅝	4⅜	4-1
1½	7	1¼	3¼	1¾	1¾	4⅞	4-1⅛
2	8½	1½	4	2¼	2¼	6½	8-1
2½	9⅝	1⅝	4⅛	2½	2½	7½	8-1⅛
3	9½	1½	4	2⅛	2⅛	7½	8-1
3½	..	..	..	..	..	..	..
4	11½	1¾	4½	2¾	2¾	9¼	8-1¼
5	13¾	2	5	3⅛	3⅛	11	8-1⅜
6	15	2 3/16	5½	3⅜	3⅜	12½	12-1¼
8	18½	2½	6⅜	4	4½	15½	12-1½
10	21½	2¾	7¼	4¼	5	18½	16-1½
12	24	3⅛	7⅞	4⅝	5⅝	21	20-1½
14	25¼	3⅜	8⅜	5⅛	6⅛	22	20-1⅝
16	27¾	3½	8½	5¼	6½	24¼	20-1¾
18	31	4	9	6	7½	27	20-2
20	33¾	4¼	9¾	6¼	8¼	29½	20-2⅛
24	41	5½	11½	8	10½	35½	20-2⅝

1500 LB. FLANGES

Nom. Pipe Size	O	C②	Y② Weld Neck	Y② Slip on Thrd.	Y② Lap Joint	Bolt Circle	No. and Size of Holes
½	4¾	⅞	2⅜	1¼	1¼	3¼	4-⅞
¾	5⅛	1	2¾	1⅜	1⅜	3½	4-⅞
1	5⅞	1⅛	2⅞	1⅝	1⅝	4	4-1
1¼	6¼	1⅛	2⅞	1⅝	1⅝	4⅜	4-1
1½	7	1¼	3¼	1¾	1¾	4⅞	4-1⅛
2	8½	1½	4	2¼	2¼	6½	8-1
2½	9⅝	1⅝	4⅛	2½	2½	7½	8-1⅛
3	10½	1⅞	4⅝	2⅞	2⅞	8	8-1¼
3½	..	..	..	..	..	..	..
4	12¼	2⅛	4⅞	3 9/16	3 9/16	9½	8-1⅜
5	14¾	2⅞	6⅛	4⅛	4⅛	11½	8-1⅝
6	15½	3¼	6¾	4 11/16	4 11/16	12½	12-1½
8	19	3⅝	8⅜	5⅝	5⅝	15½	12-1¾
10	23	4¼	10	6¼	7	19	12-2
12	26½	4⅞	11⅛	7⅛	8⅝	22½	16-2⅛
14	29½	5¼	11¾	..	9½	25	16-2⅜
16	32½	5¾	12¼	..	10¼	27¾	16-2⅝
18	36	6⅜	12⅞	..	10⅞	30½	16-2⅞
20	38¾	7	14	..	11½	32¾	16-3⅛
24	46	8	16	..	13	39	16-3⅝

2500 LB. FLANGES

Nom. Pipe Size	O	C②	Y② Weld Neck	Y② Slip on Thrd.	Y② Lap Joint	Bolt Circle	No. and Size of Holes
½	5¼	1 3/16	2⅞	1 9/16	1 9/16	3½	4-⅞
¾	5½	1¼	3⅛	1 11/16	1 11/16	3¾	4-⅞
1	6¼	1⅜	3½	1⅞	1⅞	4¼	4-1
1¼	7¼	1½	3¾	2 1/16	2 1/16	5⅛	4-1⅛
1½	8	1¾	4⅜	2⅜	2⅜	5¾	4-1¼
2	9¼	2	5	2¾	2¾	6¾	8-1⅛
2½	10½	2¼	5⅝	3⅛	3⅛	7¾	8-1¼
3	12	2⅝	6⅝	3⅝	3⅝	9	8-1⅜
4	14	3	7½	4¼	4¼	10¾	8-1⅝
5	16½	3⅝	9	5⅛	5⅛	12¾	8-1⅞
6	19	4¼	10¾	6	6	14½	8-2⅛
8	21¾	5	12½	7	7	17¼	12-2⅛
10	26½	6½	16½	9	9	21¼	12-2⅝
12	30	7¼	18¼	10	10	24⅜	12-2⅞

WELDING NECK FLANGE BORES①③

Nom. Pipe Size	Outside Diam.	Light Wall⑥	Sched. 20	Sched. 30	Std. Wall.	Sched. 40	Sched. 60	Extra Strong	Sched. 80	Sched. 100	Sched. 120	Sched. 140	Sched. 160	Double Extra Strong
½	0.840	.674	...	...	0.622	0.622	...	0.546	0.546	...	...	...	0.464	0.252
¾	1.050	.884	...	...	0.824	0.824	...	0.742	0.742	...	...	...	0.612	0.434
1	1.315	1.097	...	...	1.049	1.049	...	0.957	0.957	...	...	...	0.815	0.599
1¼	1.660	1.442	...	...	1.380	1.380	...	1.278	1.278	...	...	...	1.160	0.896
1½	1.900	1.682	...	...	1.610	1.610	...	1.500	1.500	...	...	...	1.338	1.100
2	2.375	2.157	...	...	2.067	2.067	...	1.939	1.939	...	...	...	1.687	1.503
2½	2.875	2.635	...	...	2.469	2.469	...	2.323	2.323	...	...	...	2.125	1.771
3	3.500	3.260	...	...	3.068	3.068	...	2.900	2.900	...	...	...	2.624	2.300
3½	4.000	3.760	...	...	3.548	3.548	...	3.364	3.364	...	...	...	...	2.728
4	4.500	4.260	...	...	4.026	4.026	...	3.826	3.826	...	3.624	...	3.438	3.152
5	5.563	5.295	...	...	5.047	5.047	...	4.813	4.813	...	4.563	...	4.313	4.063
6	6.625	6.357	...	...	6.065	6.065	...	5.761	5.761	...	5.501	...	5.187	4.897
8	8.625	8.329	8.125	8.071	7.981	7.981	7.813	7.625	7.625	7.437	7.187	7.001	6.813	6.875
10	10.750	10.420	10.250	10.136	10.020	10.020	9.750	9.750	9.562	9.312	9.062	8.750	8.500	8.750
12	12.750	12.390	12.250	12.090	12.000	11.938	11.626	11.750	11.374	11.062	10.750	10.500	10.126	10.750
14	14.000	13.500	13.376	13.250	13.250	13.124	12.812	13.000	12.500	12.124	11.814	11.500	11.188	...
16	16.000	15.500	15.376	15.250	15.250	15.000	14.688	15.000	14.312	13.938	13.564	13.124	12.812	...
18	18.000	17.500	17.376	17.124	17.250	16.876	16.500	17.000	16.124	15.688	15.250	14.876	14.438	...
20	20.000	19.500	19.250	19.000	19.250	18.812	18.376	19.000	17.938	17.438	17.000	16.500	16.062	...
24	24.000	23.500	23.250	22.876	23.250	22.624	22.062	23.000	21.562	20.938	20.376	19.876	19.312	...
30	30.000	29.376	29.000	28.750	29.250	...	...	29.000	...	...	...	...	...	...
36	36.000	35.376	35.000	34.750	35.250	34.500	...	35.000	...	...	...	...	...	...
42	42.000	...	...	...	41.250	...	...	41.000	...	...	...	...	...	...
48	48.000	...	...	...	47.250	...	...	47.000	...	...	...	...	...	...

NOTES:

① Always specify bore when ordering.

② Includes 1/16" raised face in 150 lb. and 300 lb. standards. Does **not** include 1/4" raised face in 400 lb. and heavier standards.

③ Inside pipe diameters are also provided by this table.

④ Other types, sizes and facings on application.

⑤ Stocked in carbon steel and a variety of other metals and alloys.

⑥ Light Wall diameters are identical to stainless steel Schedule 10S in sizes thru 12", and to Schedule 10 in sizes 14" and larger.

Fig. B-2. Chart of ANSI Forged Steel Flanges. (Taylor-Bonney Div., Gulf + Western Mfg. Co.)

APPENDIX C
VENDORS' VALVE DATA

This appendix presents a sampling of pages taken from vendor catalogs. The information they contain is used in several problems and exercises. Familiarize yourself with the kinds of valves found here and the types of dimensions used.

NAMES OF PARTS

gate

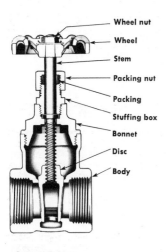

Wheel nut
Wheel
Stem
Packing nut
Packing
Stuffing box
Bonnet
Disc
Body

**Gate, N-R Stem
Screwed Bonnet
Wedge Disc**

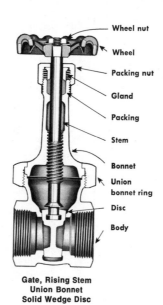

Wheel nut
Wheel
Packing nut
Gland
Packing
Stem
Bonnet
Union bonnet ring
Disc
Body

**Gate, Rising Stem
Union Bonnet
Solid Wedge Disc**

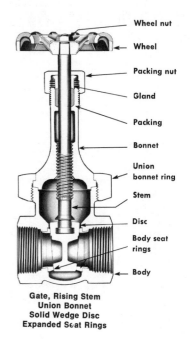

Wheel nut
Wheel
Packing nut
Gland
Packing
Bonnet
Union bonnet ring
Stem
Disc
Body seat rings
Body

**Gate, Rising Stem
Union Bonnet
Solid Wedge Disc
Expanded Seat Rings**

globe

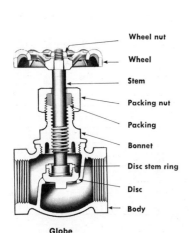

Wheel nut
Wheel
Stem
Packing nut
Packing
Bonnet
Disc stem ring
Disc
Body

**Globe
Screwed Bonnet
Metal Disc**

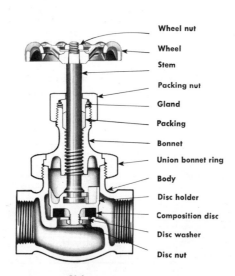

Wheel nut
Wheel
Stem
Packing nut
Gland
Packing
Bonnet
Union bonnet ring
Body
Disc holder
Composition disc
Disc washer
Disc nut

**Globe
Union Bonnet
Composition or TFE Disc**

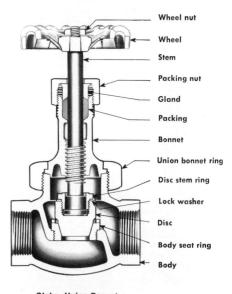

Wheel nut
Wheel
Stem
Packing nut
Gland
Packing
Bonnet
Union bonnet ring
Disc stem ring
Lock washer
Disc
Body seat ring
Body

**Globe, Union Bonnet
Plug Type Disc
Renewable Seat Rings**

Crane

IRON WEDGE GATE VALVES

125-POUND FERROSTEEL WEDGE GATE
Bronze Trimmed or All-Iron

Non-Rising Stem

Threaded
No. 460
Bronze Trimmed

Flanged
No. 461
Bronze Trimmed

No. 473
All-Iron

Outside Screw & Yoke

Threaded
No. 464½
Bronze Trimmed

Flanged
No. 465
Bronze Seats, Steel Stem

No. 465½
Bronze Seats, Bronze Stem

No. 475½
All-Iron

Sizes 10" and larger have conventional stuffing box

OS & Y Valve
Illustrated

RATINGS

Temp.	Psi, Non-Shock			
F	2 to 12"	14 & 16"	18 to 24"	30 to 48"
−20 to 150°	200	150	150	150
200	190	145	135	115
225	180	140	130	100
250	175	140	125	85
275	170	135	120	65
300	165	130	110	50
325	155	130	105	*
350	150	125	100	*
375	145	*	*	*
400	140	*	*	*
425	130	*	*	*
450	125	*	*	*

*Use Crane 150-pound steel valves.

All valves 8" and smaller have an injection type stuffing box; permits adding fresh packing with twist of a wrench. There's no need to disassemble valve or shut down the line. Outside screw and yoke valves, as shown above, also feature a modified t-head disc-stem connection within, rather than above, the disc.

Body and bonnet are Ferrosteel (ASTM A126, Class B) in sizes 16" and smaller and High Tensile Cast Iron (ASTM A126, Class C) in sizes 18" and larger.

Sizes 8-inch and smaller have injection type stuffing box. Permits adding packing with twist of a wrench at any time . . . even when valve under full rated line pressure. Turning the packing injector screw forces packing from injector reservoir into stuffing box. The packing (TFE impregnated asbestos) forms a tight seal around the stem, is self-lubricating, stays soft and pliable. When reservoir supply is depleted, insert a fresh packing stick.

In addition, non-rising stem valves feature a patented thrust collar design. The collar is above the stuffing box, completely isolated from damaging effects of line fluid. Design assures easier operation and reduced maintenance.

Sizes 10" and larger have conventional type stuffing box filled with high grade asbestos packing and equipped with a gland (bronze or nickel-plated steel, depending on trim) and malleable iron gland flange. Valves can be backseated.

Bronze Trimmed

For steam, water, air and non-corrosive oil or gas lines.

Body seat rings, screwed into the body, are bronze. Stem is bronze (except No. 465 stem is steel, nickel-plated all over). Sizes 3" and smaller have a solid bronze disc; in larger sizes, bronze disc faces are rolled into the disc. Non-rising stem valves 12" and smaller have bronze bushings above and below the stem collar.

All-Iron

For oil or gas, or for fluids that corrode bronze but not iron. Seats are cast integral with body and disc. Stem is steel, nickel-plated all over. Non-rising stem valves have steel bushings above and below the stem collar.

Compliance with Standards

All valves conform to MSS Standard SP-70. Flanged valves have ANSI B16.10, Class 125 iron wedge gate face-to-face dimensions. End flanges conform to ANSI B16.1, Class 125.

All bronze trimmed valves 12" and smaller (except No. 465) meet Federal Spec. WW-V-58b, Type I, Class 1 material and design requirements.

Size	2"	2½"	3"	3½"	4"	5"	6"	8"	10"	12"	14"	16"	18"	20"	24"	30"	36"	42"	48"
Weights																			
No. 460	26	36	45	...	76	...	...	...	...	...	...	...	...	...	...	...	...	...	...
No. 461	31	45	57	...	95	130	160	275	490	700	850	1180	1440	1740	2774		—on request—		
No. 473	33	45	57	...	95	...	160	275	...	...	...	...	...	...	...	...	...	...	...
No. 464½	28	39	48	...	80	...	...	...	...	...	...	...	...	...	...	...	...	...	...
No. 465	33	48	60	...	100	...	170	290	530	720	...	...	...	...	...	...	...	...	...
No. 465½	33	48	60	67	100	138	170	290	530	720	908	1372	1540	1950	2980	5480	9250	15000	18000
No. 475½	33	48	60	...	100	138	170	290	530	720	908	1372	1540	1950	2980	5480	9250	15000	18000
Dimensions																			
End to end	5⅜	6⅝	7	...	8	...	...	...	...	...	...	...	...	...	...	...	...	...	...
Face to face	7	7½	8	8½	9	10	10½	11½	13	14	15	16	17	18	20	24	28	33	36
Ctr. to top, N-RS	10⅛	11¾	12⅝	...	15½	17⅛	19⅝	23¾	33	36½	39½	48	49	52½	63½	76	92	106	114
Ctr. to top, OS & Y	13	15⅜	17	17	21⅝	25½	30	38	50¾	58	68	75½	83½	91½	109	138	160	191	209
Wheel dia. N-RS	6	8	8	...	10	10	12	14	20	20	20	22	24	24	30	36	42	42	42
Wheel dia. OS & Y	7	8	8	8	10	10	12	14	20	20	20	22	24	24	30	36	42	42	42

Crane

125-POUND FERROSTEEL SWING CHECK
Bronze Trimmed or All-Iron

Temp.	Psl, Non-Shock		
F	Sizes 2-12″	Sizes 14, 16″	Sizes 18-24″
—20 to 150°	200	150	150
200	190	145	135
225	180	140	130
250	175	140	125
275	170	135	120
300	165	130	110
325	155	130	105
350	150	125*	100
375	145	...	...
400	140	...	...
425	130	...	...
450	125	...	...

RATINGS

*Maximum is 125 psi saturated steam (353 F).

Valves 8″ and Smaller
(partial section)
Straight-thru body design and wide hinge support provide turbulence-free flow and accurate seating. Interior is contoured for smooth flow without undue pressure drop. Design also facilitates conversion to outside lever and weight operation...can be done in field if necessary.

Sturdy, well constructed valves. Bodies, oval or globular in shape, provide ample flow area around disc when valve is wide open. Disc cannot stick in open position. Tapped and plugged opening in each of two bosses on body provide easy access to either end of hinge ... simplify field-changeover to lever and weight operation.

Bodies 8″ and smaller have straight-thru inlet port and long sweeping contour in outlet port. Design assures unusually efficient flow characteristics.

Body and cap are Crane Ferrosteel (ASTM A126, Class B) in sizes 16″ and smaller and High Tensile Cast Iron (ASTM A126, Class C) in sizes 18″ and larger.

Bronze Trimmed

For steam, water, non-corrosive oil and gas, and other fluids that do not corrode bronze.

Body seat ring is bronze. Hinge pin, also bronze, rides in two bronze bushings, one at each side of valve body. Disc is bronze in sizes 6″ and smaller and iron faced with bronze in larger sizes.

All-Iron

For gas, oil, and fluids that corrode bronze but not iron.

Seating surfaces are cast integral with the body and disc. Exelloy hinge pin is supported by an iron bushing at each end of valve body.

Lever and Weight Valve

No. 383 except for its lever and weight mechanism is identical to the No. 373. Generally used where quick action is necessary to avoid sudden reversal of flow, to assist disc in closing, or to balance disc so that valves open with minimum pressure. They are not intended to be used as back pressure valves, unloading valves, etc.

Positioning and setting of lever and weight are easily accomplished in field. Lever can be rotated through 360° and is adjustable in 15° increments.

Installation

Crane swing check valves may be used in a horizontal position ... or in a vertical position for upward flow.

Standards

Face-to-face dimensions of flanged valves, in sizes applicable, conform to those listed in ANSI B16.10 for Class 125 cast iron swing check valves.

Dimensions and drilling of end flanges conform to ANSI B16.1, Class 125 requirements. Flanges are plain faced, with a smooth finish.

Threaded
No. 372, Bronze Trimmed
No. 372½, All-Iron

Flanged
No. 373, Bronze Trimmed
No. 373½, All-Iron
No. 383, Bronze Trimmed
With Lever & Weight
(not illustrated)

Illustration typical of sizes 10″ and larger

Crane

Size		2″	2½″	3″	4″	5″	6″	8″	10″	12″	14″	16″	18″	20″	24″
Weights	No. 372	18	22	29	54	...	...	...	...	...	...	...	...	...	...
	No. 372½	18	...	29	54	...	...	...	...	...	...	...	...	...	...
	No. 373	25	34	44	75	103	127	230	440	660	960	1420	1575	2170	3000
	No. 373½	25	34	44	75	...	127	230	440	660	...	...	...	...	...
	No. 383	30	40	54	85	...	137	240	475	710	...	...	...	...	...
Dimensions	End to end, threaded	6⅛	7¼	8	9¼	...	...	...	...	...	...	...	...	...	...
	Face to face, flanged	8	8½	9½	11½	13	14	19½	24½	27½	31	36	36	40	48
	Center to top	4½	5⅜	5⅞	6⅝	7¾	8¼	10¼	12	13¾	16	18	17½	19½	20½

SAFETY AND RELIEF VALVES

BRONZE POP SAFETY VALVES
For Steam

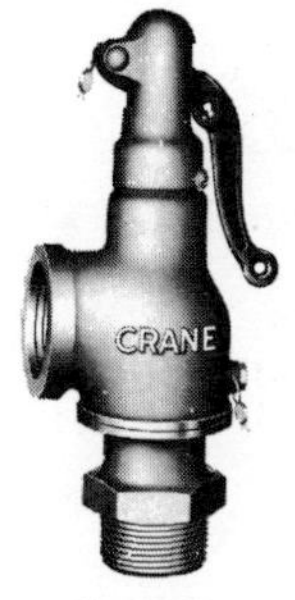

No. 2501
Side Outlet

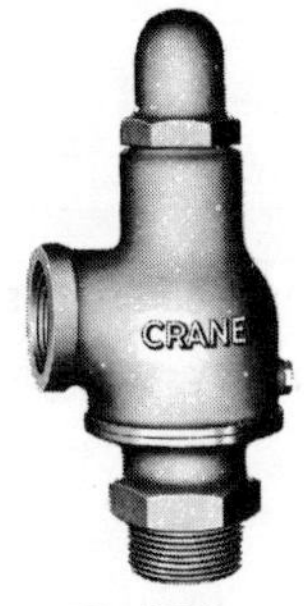

No. 2601
Side Outlet

Recommended for steam service on boilers, miniature boilers, and unfired pressure vessels such as receivers, pipe lines, etc.

No. 2501 complies with requirements of the ASME Power Boiler Code (Section I), Miniature Boiler Code (Section V), and Unfired Pressure Vessel Code (Section VIII). A wire seal prevents tampering with the factory pressure setting.

No. 2601 are widely used in non-Code installations. They are pressure-tight on the outlet side and can discharge against low back pressures. A stuffing box around the spring adjusting screw is filled with asbestos packing to form an effective seal for the body.

BRONZE POP SAFETY VALVES
For Air and Gas

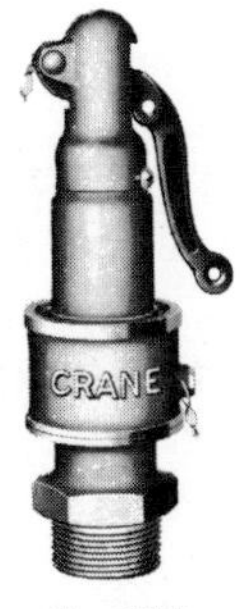

No. 2550
Top Discharge

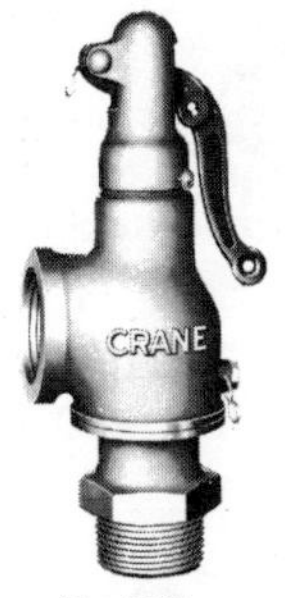

No. 2551
Side Outlet

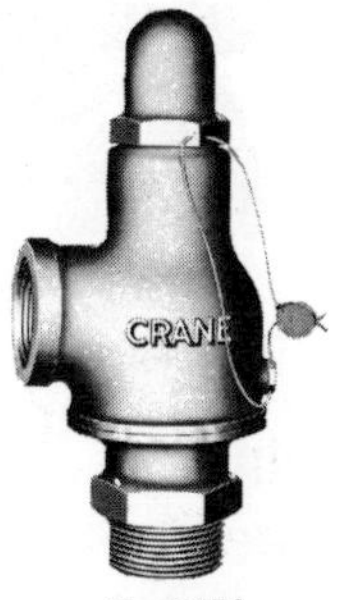

No. 2651
Side Outlet

Recommended for air and gas service on receivers, tanks, pipe lines, compressors, cylinders, etc.

Nos. 2551 and 2651 are preferred for gas service because their side outlet permits the discharge to be piped away. For noxious or inflammable gases, however, use the No. 2651. It is pressure-tight on outlet side, can discharge against low back pressures, and a stuffing box around the spring adjusting screw is filled with asbestos packing to form an effective seal for the body.

The valves are sealed to prevent tampering with the factory pressure setting. All three comply with ASME Unfired Pressure Vessel Code, Section VIII (No. 2651 also meets noxious and inflammable gas requirements).

BRONZE SAFETY RELIEF VALVE
For Water, Oil, or Steam

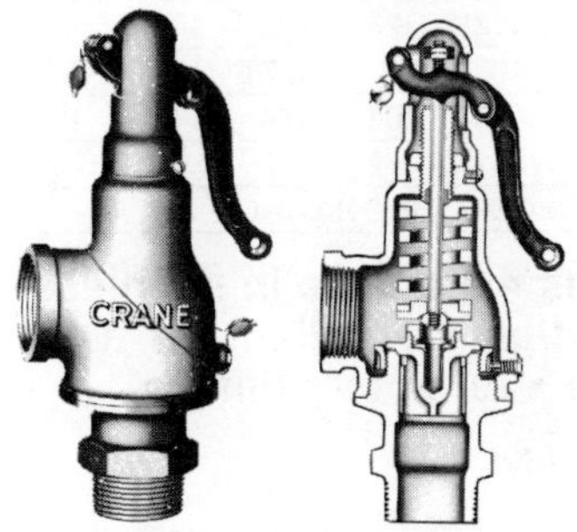

No. 2606, Side Outlet

For liquid and saturated steam service. Especially recommended for use on water heaters requiring a valve of outstanding quality.

Has a pop chamber and blowdown regulating ring which effect the same positive operating action as a pop safety valve should steam develop in water heater. Stuffing box around stem prevents leakage of hot water from top of valve. Wire seal prevents tampering with factory pressure setting.

Complies with ASME Unfired Pressure Vessel Code, Section VIII.

BRONZE RELIEF VALVE
For Water or Oil

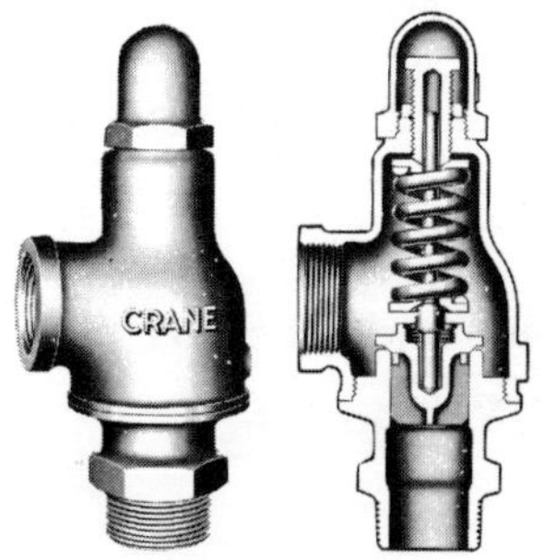

No. 2611, Side Outlet

For liquid service on pipe lines, cylinders, presses, pumps, etc. Relief valves are intended to relieve excessive pressures; however they should not be used in an attempt to relieve shock pressures in hydraulic lines.

Valves are pressure-tight on outlet side and can discharge against low head pressures. Stuffing box around main spring adjusting screw is filled with asbestos packing to seal body area.

Complies with ASME Unfired Pressure Vessel Code, Section VIII.

WEIGHTS AND DIMENSIONS

Size (inlet)	Weight	Dimensions, Inches				
Inches	Pounds Each	Center of stem to end of side outlet	Center of side outlet to top of cap	Over-all height to top of cap	Over-all height to top of lever, open	Size of side outlet
No. 2501						
⅜	0.8	1⅛	3¾	6	7⅝	½
½	1.0	1⅛	3¾	6	7⅝	½
¾	2.0	1⅜	3¾	6½	8¼	¾
1	3.0	1⅝	4⅝	7⅞	9¾	1
1¼	4.0	1¾	4⅜	7⅞	9¾	1¼
1½	5.0	2⅛	5¼	9⅛	11⅜	1½
2	8.0	2 7/16	6⅛	10⅝	13½	2
2½	13.0	2⅞	7¾	12¾	16	2½
No. 2550						
⅜	0.8	...	...	6	7⅝	...
½	1.0	...	...	6	7⅝	...
¾	2.0	...	...	6½	8¼	...
1	3.0	...	...	7⅞	9¾	...
No. 2551						
⅜	0.8	1⅛	3¾	6	7⅝	½
½	1.0	1⅛	3¾	6	7⅝	½
¾	2.0	1⅜	3¾	6½	8¼	¾
1	3.0	1⅝	4⅝	7⅞	9¾	1
No. 2601, 2611, 2651						
⅜	1.0	1⅛	3⅛	5⅜	...	½
½	1.2	1⅛	3⅛	5⅜	...	½
¾	2.0	1⅜	3¼	6	...	¾
1	3.0	1⅝	3⅝	6⅞	...	1
No. 2606						
½	1.0	1⅛	3¾	6	7⅝	½
¾	1.7	1⅜	3¾	6½	8¼	¾
1	2.8	1⅝	4⅝	7⅞	9¾	1

Crane

VALVE SIZE	3	4	6	8	10	12	14	16	18	20	24
Face to Face	9½	11½	14	19½	24½	27½	31	34	38½	38½	51
Centerline to Top	6¼	7	8¾	10¼	12½	14½	14½	16⅜	18	20½	25
Centerline to Shaft	2⅜	3½	5⅛	5¾	7⅛	8½	8½	9½	10¾	12	15
Weight	35	57	95	168	240	405	460	675	820	1010	1300

VALVE SIZE	30	36	42	48
Face to Face	50	60	66	72
Centerline to Top	31	39	44	50
Centerline to Shaft	19	22½	27	30
Weight	2700	3600	4700	6300

DIMENSIONS SHOWN FOR 50 LB. C.W.P. OVER 24″ SIZE

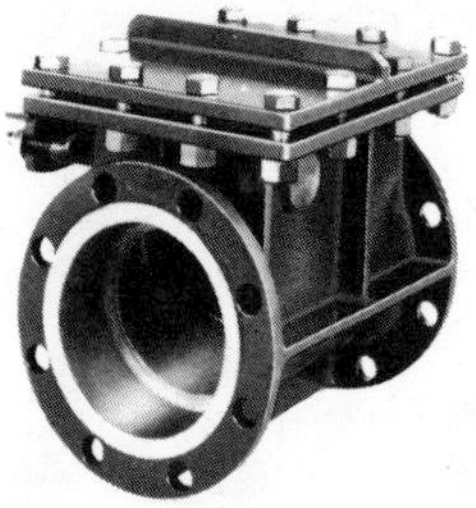

FIG. 10

Swing Check Valve

Easily cleaned while in line • adjustable counterweight to control slamming • 150 lb. C.W.P.

VALVE SIZE	3	4	6	8	10	12	14	16	18	20	24
Face to Face	9½	11½	14	18	21¾	25½	28	29½	31	32½	39½
Bolt Circle	6	7½	9½	11¾	14¼	17	18¾	21¾	22¾	25	29½
Flange Diameter	7½	9	11	13½	16	19	21	23½	25	27½	32
Number of Holes	4	8	8	8	12	12	12	16	16	20	20
Hole Size	¾	¾	⅞	⅞	1	1	1⅛	1⅛	1¼	1¼	1⅜
Weight	40	50	70	130	190	280	370	470	550	640	1100

Drip-free shutoff • easily disassembled for cleaning and maintenance • 150 lb. C.W.P. • stop check valve available.

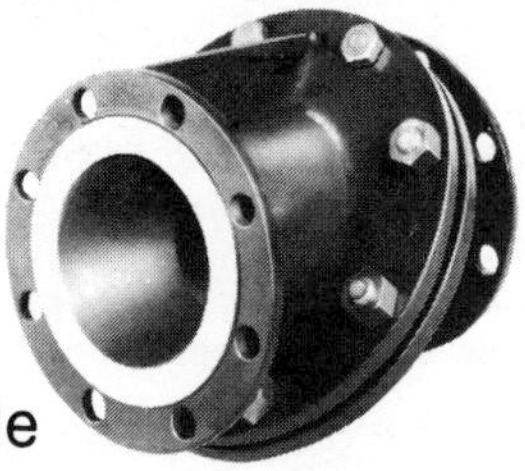

FIG. 11

Angle Disc Check Valve

VALVE SIZE	24	30	36	42	48	54	60	72	84	96	108	120	132	144
Face to Face	8	12	12	12	15	15	15	18	18	18	24	24	24	24
Flange Diameter	32	38¾	46	53	59½	66¼	73	86½	99¾	113¼	124	132	144	162
Bolt Circle Diameter	29½	36	42¾	49½	56	62¾	69¼	82½	95½	108½	120	127½	139½	157
Number of Bolts	20	28	32	36	44	44	52	60	64	68	108	144	144	96
Bolt Size	¾	⅞	⅞	1	1	1¼	1¼	1¼	1½	1¾	2	2	2	2
Weight	WEIGHTS VARY WITH PRESSURE AND TEMPERATURE RATING													

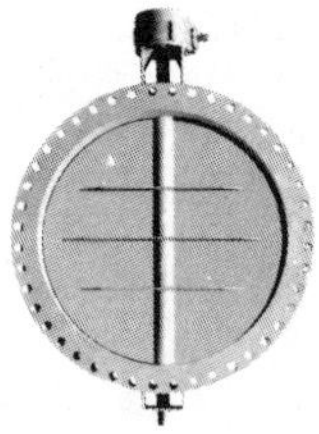

FIG. 50

Flanged Butterfly Valve

Lightweight • economical • seat designs for all applications • available in stainless steel and other alloys • custom designed to meet application • excellent for high temperature service to 2000°F • rectangular types available • refractory linings.

VALVE SIZE	2	3	4	6	8	10	12	14	16	18	20	24
Face to Face	1⅞	2	2	2¼	2¾	2¾	3	3	3½	3½	4½	4½
Flange Diameter	6	7½	9	11	13½	16	19	21	23½	25	27½	32
Bolt Circle	4¾	6	7½	9½	11¾	14¼	17	18¾	21¼	22¾	25	29½
Number of Bolts	4	4	8	8	8	12	12	12	16	16	20	20
Bolt Size Tap NC	⅝	⅝	⅝	¾	¾	⅞	⅞	1	1	1⅛	1⅛	1¼
Center to Top, Open	17⅛	20½	22⅝	28⅝	37	42¾	49⅛	50⅛	57⅞	64	70½	82⅝
Handwheel Diameter	8	10	10	12	16	16	18	18	24	24	24	30
Weight	30	33	37	59	105	145	205	235	320	390	515	690

Solid one-piece cast body • O-ring seating available • Neoprene and asbestos packing for maximum sealing • available in titanium • 150 lb. C.W.P.

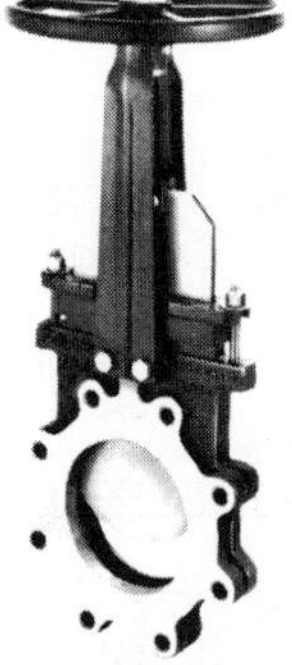

FIG. 45

Cast Knife Gate Valve

Fabri-Valve

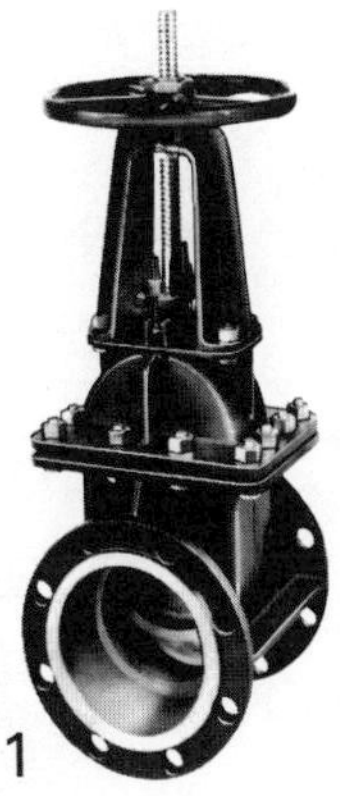

VALVE SIZE	2	3	4	5	6	8	10	12	14	16	18	20	24
Face to Face	7	8	9	10	10½	11½	13	14	15	16	17	18	20
Handwheel Diameter	8	10	10	12	12	16	16	18	18	24	24	24	30
Centerline to Top, Open	16½	19½	23	27	31	40½	46¾	55¼	55¼	67	73½	77¼	92¼
Weight	36	55	70	80	100	175	230	330	400	550	650	750	1200

VALVE SIZE	30	36	42	48	54	60	72	84	96
Face to Face	24	28	33	36	39	42	48	—	—
Handwheel Diameter	30	36	MANUAL OR ELECTRIC GEAR OPERATORS						
Centerline to Top, Open	128	150	174	198				DIMENSIONS AVAILABLE	
Weight	2200	2600	3700	4800	6800	8800	10400	14800	19200 ON APPLICATION

DIMENSIONS AND WEIGHTS VARY WITH PRESSURE RATING OVER 24″ SIZE

FIG. 71

Wedge Gate Valve

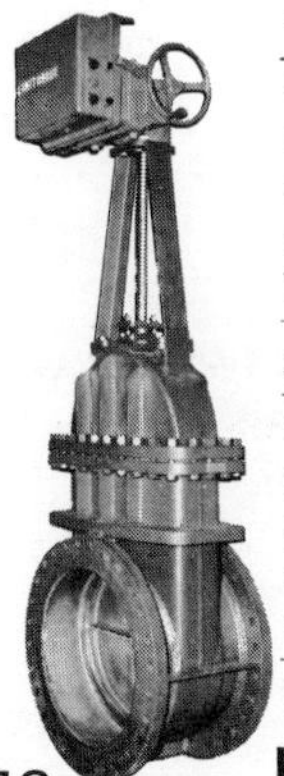

Wedge gate assures positive shutoff · fabricated from any weldable alloy · sizes through 96″ · standard working pressure is 150 lb. C.W.P. · other working pressure designs available.

150 lb. Working Pressure

VALVE SIZE	10	12	14	16	18	20	24	30	36	42	48	54	60
Face to Face	13	14	15	16	17	18	20	24	28	33	36	39	42
Handwheel Diameter	16	18	18	24	24	24	30	Manual or Electric Gear Operators Recommended					
Center to Top Open	46¹³⁄₁₆	55¼	61	69¾	78½	84¾	100⅝	123	144	165	186		
Weight (lb.)	370	435	660	875	1000	1320	1700	3450	4900	7100	9600	13200	18000

300 lb. Working Pressure

VALVE SIZE	10	12	14	16	18	20	24	30	36	42	48	54	60
Face to Face	18	19¾	30	33	36	39	45	55	UPON APPLICATION				
Handwheel diameter	MANUAL OR ELECTRIC GEAR OPERATORS												
Center to Top Open	51	60½	67	76	84½	90¼	110	132					
Weight (lb.)	670	780	1150	1575	1900	2500	3225	6550	9300	13300	18300	25000	34000

Flanges 24″ and smaller per ANSI B-16.5   26″ to 60″ per API 605

**FIG. 78
Heavy Duty Wedge Gate Valve**

Pressure ratings meet ANSI B16.5 requirements · fabricated of combined wrought plate and castings ASTM rated · other alloy trim, replaceable seats, lantern stuffing box optionally available · welders qualified per ASME Section IX · positive shutoff · fully welded seats · single floating disc · fully machined back seat allows valve to be repacked under pressure · fully machined raised face on flanges · valve tested in accordance with MSS SP-61.

VALVE SIZE	2	3	4	5	6	8	10	12	14	16	18	20	24
Face to Face	1⅞	2	2	2¼	2¼	2¾	2¾	3	3	3½	3½	4½	4½
Handwheel Diameter	8	10	10	12	12	16	16	18	18	24	24	24	30
Centerline to Top, Open	22	24¼	27½	32	35¼	45¼	52¼	62½	62½	73½	81	90	103
Weight	40	61	77	89	110	190	260	370	440	600	715	825	1300

VALVE SIZE	30	36	42	48	54	60	72	84	96
Face to Face	3⅝	4⅛	5	5½					
Handwheel Diameter	30	36	MANUAL OR ELECTRIC GEAR OPERATORS						
Centerline to Top, Open	106	140	177	189				DIMENSIONS AVAILABLE	
Weight	1850	2550	3450	4700	5950	7350	10600	14400	19600 ON APPLICATION

DIMENSIONS AND WEIGHTS VARY WITH PRESSURE RATING OVER 24″ SIZE
DIMENSIONS SHOWN FOR 50 LB. C.W.P. OVER 24″ SIZE

Knife gate assures positive, non-clogging shutoff on suspended solids · bonnet design eliminates leakage through the packing gland · O-ring seating available for drip-tight shutoff sizes to 96″ · 150 lb. C.W.P. standard · Other working pressure designs available.

**FIG. 134
Bonnet-type Knife Gate Valve**

Fabri-Valve

ACTUATORS

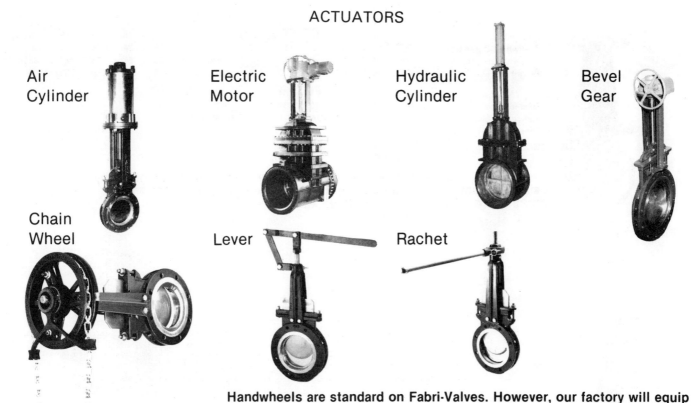

Air Cylinder

Electric Motor

Hydraulic Cylinder

Bevel Gear

Chain Wheel

Lever

Rachet

Handwheels are standard on Fabri-Valves. However, our factory will equip your valves with any type of actuator you specify. We can supply a wide variety of actuators, depending on valve size and service.

INSTRUMENTATION

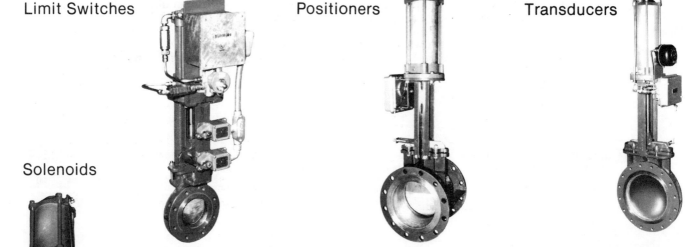

Limit Switches

Positioners

Transducers

Solenoids

Fabri-Valve will install instrumentation at the factory—and save you time and installation costs. Our cylinder actuated valves can be equipped with four-way solenoids for remote operations; positioners for automatic control; limit switches to indicate open and closed position; position transmitters; transducers; cylinder speed control valves; and fail-safe systems.

Fabri-Valve

GATES

Solid Wedge • Multiple Bolted Bonnet
Outside Screw & Yoke • Rising Spindle

Screwed: 200 lbs., 500° F.

Flanged: 150 lbs., 500° F.
230 lbs., –20° F. to 100° F.

Fig. 1324
1/4" and 3/8"

Fig. 1324, 1/2"-2"
Fig. 2324, 1/2"-1"

Fig. 1325, 1/2"-1 1/2"
Fig. 2325, 1" and 1 1/2"

Figs. 1325 or 2325
2"-4"

Figs. 1325 or 2325
6" and 8"

FIGURES 1324 AND 1325 are made of Type 316 alloy; Figs. 2324 and 2325 are made of Type J-20 alloy. They embody gate valve construction features which assure long, trouble-free valve performance in lines where severe corrosive conditions prevail.

Through-port design permits full, unobstructed flow when valve is wide open, minimizing turbulence.

Sturdy, solid wedge, slotted for engagement to Tee head of spindle, is held in position by body guide ribs. This reduces drag and wear on the seat, and lessens chatter in rapidly vibrating currents.

Rising spindle serves as indicator of wedge position. Threads are outside of valve, away from corrosive media in the line and are easily accessible for lubricating and cleaning.

Multiple bolted bonnet assures tight body-bonnet joint and permits easy and repeated dismantling for cleaning inside of valve or renewal of parts.

Deep packing box has chevron-type Teflon packing, especially suitable for corrosive services.

Each valve is individually tested for tightness and subjected to a 300 psi hydrostatic shell test and a 200 psi seat test.

Dimensions

Size, in.	1/4	3/8	1/2	3/4	1	1 1/4	1 1/2	2	2 1/2	3	4	6	8
Diameter of Wheel	3	3	3 1/2	3 1/2	4	4 3/8	4 7/8	7	7	8	10	12	14
Figs. 1324 or 2324:													
Center to Spindle Top .... OPEN	-------	-------	6 5/8	7 9/16	9	9 3/4	11 5/16	15	-------	-------	-------	-------	-------
Center to Wheel Top	6 1/2	6 1/2	5 11/16	6 7/16	7 5/8	8 1/4	9 7/16	12 1/4	-------	-------	-------	-------	-------
End to End	1 3/4	2 1/4	2 3/4	3 1/16	3 1/2	3 7/8	4 5/16	4 9/16	-------	-------	-------	-------	-------
Figs. 1325 or 2325:													
Center to Spindle Top .... OPEN	-------	-------	6 3/4	7 11/16	9 1/8	10	11 5/16	15	16 5/8	18 1/2	21 3/4	29 5/8	37
Center to Wheel Top	-------	-------	5 13/16	6 9/16	7 3/4	8 3/8	9 7/16	12 1/4	13 1/4	14 5/8	17 1/4	23	28 1/4
Face to Face	-------	-------	4 1/4	4 5/8	5	5 1/2	6 1/2	7	7 1/2	8	9	10 1/2	11 1/2
Flange Diameter	-------	-------	3 1/2	3 7/8	4 1/4	4 5/8	5	6	7	7 1/2	9	11	13 1/2
Flange Thickness	-------	-------	3/8	13/32	7/16	1/2	9/16	5/8	11/16	3/4	15/16	1	1 1/8

Jenkins

GLOBES

Regrinding Beveled Disc and Seat • Bolted Bonnet
Outside Screw & Yoke • Rising Spindle

Screwed: 200 lbs., 500° F.

Flanged: 150 lbs., 500° F.
230 lbs., –20° F. to 100° F.

Fig. 1316-A

Fig. 1317-A, ½"-3"

Fig. 1317-A, 4" and 6"

Figures 1316-A and 1317-A made of Type 316 alloy are recommended for controlling corrosive gases or fluids where conditions are severe, where the close regulation feature of a globe valve is essential and where spindle threads must be out of the line of flow.

Outside screw and yoke design permits spindle threads to be easily cleaned and lubricated. Rising spindle and wheel serve as indicator of disc position.

Multiple bolted bonnet with male and female body-bonnet joint assures tightness and permits easy dismantling for cleaning or removal of parts.

A hole in the spindle, with corresponding grooves in the disc locknut through which a pin is inserted, enables the spindle-disc assembly to be used for regrinding when necessary.

Packing box is deep, holding a liberal quantity of Teflon ring packing.

Each valve is tested for tightness and subjected to a 300 psi hydrostatic shell test and a 200 psi seat test.

Dimensions

Size, in.	½	¾	1	1½	2	2½	3	4	6
Center to Wheel Top................OPEN	6⅜	6⅝	7⅝	8⅝	9⅝	12⅛	13¾	15⅞	19⅛
Diameter of Wheel...............................	3	3	3¹¹⁄₁₆	6	7	8	8	10	12
Fig. 1316-A:									
End to End..	2¾	3	3½	....	....	....	....	....	....
Fig. 1317-A:									
Face to Face..	4¼	4⅝	5	6½	8	8½	9½	11½	16
Flange Diameter	3½	3⅞	4¼	5	6	7	7½	9	11
Flange Thickness	⅜	¹³⁄₃₂	⁷⁄₁₆	⁹⁄₁₆	⅝	¹¹⁄₁₆	¾	¹⁵⁄₁₆	1

Jenkins

DICTIONARY OF TERMS

A

AGITATOR: A propeller attached to a shaft and a motor that is mounted on tanks and used to mix liquids and solutions to prevent settling of solids.

B

BALL VALVE: A regulating valve that utilizes a ball with a hole through it to adjust amount of flow through valve.

BAY: Space between two structural steel or concrete columns along side of a building.

BAY LINE: An identification number or letter given to a specific line of structural steel members that are aligned across width of a building.

BILL OF MATERIALS: A complete list of items needed to construct a tank or an assembly of pipe. Usually found on spool drawings and tank drawings.

BLIND FLANGE: A circular piece of blank plate steel having a machined face and bolt holes around perimeter. It is used to temporarily seal end of a pipe.

BOILER: A heater fired by oil, natural gas, or wood chips, used to heat or reheat water or condensate and convert it to steam.

BUTTERFLY VALVE: A valve with a rotating stem attached to a flat plate. Plate rotates 90° in place with only a quarter turn of stem.

BUTTWELD: A type of weld in which two pieces of material (pipe) are "butted" together and welded.

C

CAP: A pipe fitting that is used to seal end of a pipe.

CHAINWHEEL: A valve operator composed of a pulley wheel and a chain that is attached to gate valves located out of reach overhead.

CHECK VALVE: A valve containing a spring-operated flap that allows flow in one direction only. Flap "checks" backflow.

CLARIFIER: A large open tank, usually concrete, into which wastewater and effluent is piped. Heavy material settles to bottom and is pumped away, and clear or "clarified" liquid flows over top and is piped elsewhere for treatment.

CONCENTRIC REDUCER: A pipe fitting with different diameter openings at each end used to change size of piping run. Openings at each end have same centerline.

CONDENSER: A piece of equipment that accepts gases at one end, cools them with a refrigerant, and discharges a liquid condensate at other end.

CONSULTANT: A person or company hired by a client to design or modify systems, products, or services.

CONTROL VALVE: An automatic valve of any type that operates as a result of electric, pneumatic, hydraulic, capillary, or electromagnetic signals.

COLUMN: A vertically oriented vessel used in petrochemical industry to distill various products from crude oil. Also: a vertically oriented structural steel member used to support other steel, wood, or concrete structural elements.

COLUMN LINE: A line of structural steel columns that runs length of a building. An identification number or letter is usually assigned to a column line.

CROSS: A pipe fitting that has four openings at 90° to each other.

CUTTING PLANE LINE: A thick line that indicates where a section or elevation is to be "cut."

CYCLONE: A piece of separation equipment inside which a whirling motion is created to separate heavy solids from lighter material.

D

DOWNCOMER: A vertical pipe in which fluid is flowing down.

DRYER (ROTARY KILN): A piece of equipment resembling a long inclined tube used to dry lime slurry in pulp and paper mills.

E

ECCENTRIC REDUCER: A pipe fitting with different diameter openings at each end, and having one side that is flat. Used to reduce pipe run size in situations where one side of pipe run must remain level.

ELBOLET: A pipe fitting that is used to create a branch on an existing elbow fitting.

ELBOW: A pipe fitting that creates a bend in pipe run, usually 90° or 45°.

ELEVATION: A vertical measurement from a datum point. Used on most piping drawings to indicate vertical measurement.

EVAPORATOR: A piece of separation equipment in which water is removed or "evaporated" from a liquid chemical compound through steam heating.

EXPANDER FLANGE: A flange with an "expanded" neck that is used in place of reducers or reducing flanges to create a change in pipe run size.

F

FILTER: Any piece of equipment that removes liquid or solids from a solution.

FITTING-TO-FITTING: Several fittings attached with no pipe in between.

FLANGE: A circular piece of plate steel with a machined face, bolt holes in perimeter, and a large hole in center to match size of a piece of pipe. Used to attach valves and instruments to a pipe run.

FLOW DIAGRAM: A non-scale schematic type drawing that illustrates flow of materials through a system using symbols and various thicknesses of lines.

FLOW LINE: Thick and thin lines (primary and secondary flow) used on flow diagrams to indicate flow of substances through a system.

FLUSH-BOTTOM TANK VALVE: An angled, globe type valve used at low point of tanks to facilitate easy discharge of fluids.

G

GASKET: A thin piece of rubber or asbestos that is placed between two flanges to provide a leak-proof seal.

GATE VALVE: A valve designed for on and off service. It is actuated by turning a handwheel which raises and lowers a flat piece of metal called a gate.

GEAR OPERATOR: An operating mechanism attached to valves composed of a bevel or spur gear.

GENERAL ARRANGEMENT: A plan view drawing that shows outline of buildings, structural steel columns, equipment centerlines and outlines, and locating dimensions for major pieces of equipment.

GLOBE VALVE: A regulating valve in which a rounded or "globe" shaped mechanism is attached to a stem to make contact with valve seat.

H

HANDWHEEL: A valve operating mechanism composed of a circular wheel attached to a stem. It is turned manually to open and close valve.

HANDWHEEL EXTENSION: A mechanism attached to valve stem to extend handwheel up above walkways, platforms, and obstructions.

I

INSTRUMENT: A precisely calibrated mechanism that can sense, transmit, indicate, record, and control various process variables.

ISOMETRIC: See PIPING ISOMETRIC.

K

KNIFE GATE: A type of gate valve having a thin profile. Used in areas of limited space.

L

LAP JOINT FLANGE: A flange composed of two parts, "stub end" and flange. Used on expensive pipe such as stainless steel.

LATERAL: A pipe fitting that has a branch of run size or smaller entering run pipe at an angle such as 45°.

LATROLET: A pipe fitting that is welded to a run pipe to create a branch at an angle to run.

LOOP: An interconnected group of instruments, or a "circuit" in which one or more instruments are connected.

M

MANHOLE: An access way into tanks and vessels.

MATCH LINE: A thick line used to align or "match" two drawings together to create a complete plan or system.

MILL COORDINATES: Numbers or measurements used to locate a specific point in a plant site from a mill datum.

MILL DATUM: Origin, or reference point, at an industrial site for mill coordinate system. All linear measurements and elevations are taken from this point.

N

NEEDLE VALVE: A regulating valve in which a "needle-shaped" part is used to control flow of fluids through valve.

NOMINAL PIPE SIZE: A number that is an approximation of actual size of pipe.

NOZZLE: A piece of pipe that protrudes from a tank, vessel, or other piece of equipment. Pipes, hoses, or instruments are usually attached to nozzles.

NOZZLE SCHEDULE: A list of all nozzles that are attached to a tank. It contains diameter, projection length, and material composition of each nozzle.

NOZZLE WELD: A type of weld that is used to attach nozzles to tanks and vessels. It actually refers to a process of cutting a hole, inserting a short piece of pipe, and welding pipe to tank.

O

OFFSET: A situation in which fittings are used to shift pipe run from one location to another. A 45° elbow is often used for this purpose.

ORIFICE FLANGE: Two flanges with a plate inserted between them. Plate has a small hole in center and flanges have pressure-sensing devices inserted into tapped holes. Unit is used to measure pressure differences to calculate flow rates.

P

PAD: A constructed fitting that is used to strengthen a piece of pipe at a stub-in connection.

PIPE: A cylinder of various sizes, wall thicknesses, and materials used to transport liquids, slurries, and solutions.

PIPING AND INSTRUMENTATION DIAGRAM: A non-scale drawing that shows flow of materials through a system. P & ID may also show all equipment, instruments, and fittings used in system.

PIPING ISOMETRIC: A pictorial piping drawing that shows entire piping run in one three-dimensional view.

PIPING PLAN: A view of a piping system from above. A top view.

PIPING SPECIFICATION SYMBOL: A symbol on piping drawings placed on or near pipe that contains pipe diameter, content code, and identification number.

PROCESS: A system in which a raw material is introduced at one end and a finished product is claimed at other end.

PROCESS PIPING: Large size piping that is used in an industrial situation to handle materials used in manufacture of a product.

PROCESS VARIABLE: Characteristics of materials, such as fluids, used in industrial process. Temperature, pressure, and flow rates are common process variables.

PUMP: A piece of equipment that draws fluid in one side and discharges it from other side under pressure.

PYTHAGOREAN THEOREM: A mathematical formula, developed by Greek philosopher and mathematician Pythagoras, used for calculating length of sides of triangles.

R

REDUCER: A pipe fitting that changes diameter of pipe. See CONCENTRIC REDUCER and ECCENTRIC REDUCER.

REDUCING FLANGE: A flange that produces a change in diameter of pipe. Used in place of reducers.

REFINER: A piece of equipment having two grinding plates spinning rapidly in opposite directions. Coarse material is fed into refiner and fine material discharged.

REGULATING VALVE: A valve used for controlling or regulating amount of flow of a fluid through a pipe.

RELIEF VALVE: A valve designed to open at a specific set pressure or temperature and release liquid or gas until temperature or pressure falls below critical point.

RETURN: An elbow pipe fitting have a bend of 180°.

RISER: A vertical run of pipe in which fluid is flowing up.

ROLL: Breadth of a piping offset.

ROLLING OFFSET: An offset in which elevation of pipe has been changed in addition to position in plane.

RUN: Length of total offset in direction of pipe run.

S

SAFETY VALVE: A rapid-opening valve that permits momentary full flow of steam and other gases to release pressure on a pipe run or piece of equipment.

SET: Depth of offset.

SIGNAL: A message that is sent from an instrument to an operating mechanism. It can be electrical, pneumatic, hydraulic, capillary, or electromagnetic.

SIGNAL LEAD: Line type used on piping drawings to indicate specific types of signals.

SITE PLAN: An engineering map of an industrial site.

SLIP-ON FLANGE: A flange that slips over end of a pipe.

SOCKETWELD: A pipe connection composed of a socket into which pipe is inserted and welded.

SOCKOLET: A pipe fitting that produces a branch to accept socketwelded pipe and fittings smaller in diameter than run pipe.

SPOOL: A subassembly of pipe fittings.

SQUARING LINES: Thin projection lines used on piping isometric drawings to indicate plane of offset.

STRAIGHT TEE: A pipe fitting that produces a branch of run size or smaller.

STUB-IN: A pipe branching process in which a hole is cut into an existing pipe and a run size or smaller pipe is inserted and welded. Also called a ''nozzle weld.''

T

TANK: A piece of equipment of various shapes and sizes used for storage of liquids and solutions.

THREADOLET: A pipe fitting that produces a branch to accept threaded pipe and fittings smaller in diameter than run pipe.

TRAP: An automatic valve that collects air, water,

and gases in steam lines and discharges them without releasing steam. Also used in air lines to trap water.

TRAVEL: True length of pipe through an offset.

V

VENDOR: A company that manufactures and sells equipment, pipe, and fittings.

VESSEL: A piece of equipment of various shapes and sizes containing internal workings and components that generate some sort of chemical or physical activity.

W

WELDED SADDLE: A fitting that is placed around a stub-in to give additional strength to connection point.

WELDING NECK FLANGE: A flange with a long neck that is attached to fittings and pipe with a buttweld.

WELDOLET: A pipe fitting that produces a branch in run pipe to accept welded pipe and fittings that are smaller in diameter than run pipe. This fitting makes a 90° branch on run pipe.

DEDICATION

This book is dedicated to James C. ''Hack'' Hackathorn—a man with an encyclopedic knowledge of piping, and a human being with an inspiring love of life, and a contagious sense of humor.

INDEX